ECOLOGICAL THINKING

A New Approach to Educational Change

Shoshana Keiny

University Press of America,® Inc.
Lanham · New York · Oxford

Copyright © 2002 by
University Press of America,® Inc.
4720 Boston Way
Lanham, Maryland 20706
UPA Acquisitions Department (301) 459-3366

PO Box 317
Oxford
OX2 9RU, UK

ISBN 0-7618-2401-4 (paperback : alk. ppr.)

In memory of my parents, Joseph and Sara Bentwich, who were my first educators, and of my late husband and dear companion, with whom I continue the dialogue.

Contents

Foreword

This book aims to demonstrate an alternative approach to educational change based on *ecological thinking*. Such an approach is contrasted with one that is based on linear thinking. Through a series of case studies of change projects she has engaged with, over nearly two decades, Shoshana Keiny not only illustrates the major conceptual dimensions of this new approach. She also depicts some of the events and situations that significantly shaped their emergence in her thinking, during the course of such projects.

This is not simply another book about action research as an educational change strategy. Ever since its popular adoption by universities in many western countries, as a basis for award-bearing Continuous Professional Development courses in education, there has been a tendency to detach action research from the problems of transforming the curriculum experiences of students. All too often, it has become recast as small-scale research carried out by individual practitioners, to discover solutions to problems they identify in their work situations, with the university tutor playing the role of a commentator on the texts practitioners construct for the purposes of academic assessment. Such problems are often categorized in ways that both limit the range of solutions deemed appropriate, and who is responsible for implementing them.

For example, when such small-scale research focuses on a classroom problem, the curriculum context tends not to be viewed as part of the problem. This opens the way to making the teacher(s) responsible for solving the problem rather than those who construct the curriculum frameworks that shape teaching and learning. Hence, Keiny describes a tendency for teachers to propose solutions to 'discipline problems' in classrooms, in terms of strategies for managing behaviour, rather than strategies for enhancing motivation and engagement with respect to learning. Many of her case studies show how the latter involves re-conceptualising the relationship between learners, teachers and curriculum content, and that this implies changes in the epistemological models that shape the ways teachers mediate and represent knowledge to learners. Keiny reminds us that the curriculum conceived as an organisation of learning experiences does not always have to take the form of a syllabus. Her persistent concern is with changing education in the direction of a more learner-centered and learner-active process in which students take responsibility for organizing their own learning experiences.

Learning how to become a self-directed learner is Keiny's first dimension of learning within the educational change process. Here, however, the syllabus no longer shapes the activities of teaching. Rather "teachers have to learn" Keiny argues " to orchestrate a classroom in which students are active learners who initiate their own course of study". This is her second dimension of learning. Such learning she contends involves the development through action research of a normative framework, to guide the ways teachers intervene in classrooms, to help students take responsibility for their learning.

Through her case studies, Keiny creates an educational change scenario in which teachers, on the basis of their action research, develop the capacity to pedagogically order students' learning experiences in a self-organized form. It is a scenario in which teachers learn to pedagogically operationalize the idea of learner-centred education, and in which the curriculum is continuously being developed within this pedagogy rather than in advance of, and independently of it. Such a scenario implies that every pedagogical problem is a curriculum development problem. It also implies that not only can there be little development of the curriculum without the development of teachers' professional knowledge, but there can be little development of professional knowledge without curriculum development. This is a good example of the kind of *circular causality* that Keiny posits alongside *reflexivity* and *self-organisation* as key characteristics of *ecological thinking* about educational change.

Just as there is little point in detaching action research into classroom problems from the curriculum context of teachers' work so, the case studies in this book, demonstrate the practical significance of viewing curriculum development as an inherent characteristic of school improvement. The educational reforms driven by the *standards agenda* of governments in many 'western countries' have tended to take the prevailing curriculum frameworks for granted. These frameworks are not perceived to be part of the problems the reforms address.

Keiny's work fits what I have called *pedagogically-driven* as opposed to *standards-driven* educational change. The former starts with addressing problems as they appear to teachers in the course of teaching their students. The latter starts with attempts to address the measured short-fall between desired and actual outputs, specified as learning targets and levels of attainment. Of course, the former as Keiny's case studies illustrate so well, does not assume that the way teachers frame their pedagogical problems should be taken-for-granted. Action research is not a matter of discovering practical solutions to pre-defined problems, but of constantly reframing the problems in the light of new data and therefore illuminating new possibilities for action. Such a *reflexive* process of pedagogical development is supported by what Keiny calls *Learning Communities.*

In this book Shoshana Keiny demonstrates the potential of attempts to transform relationships between university-based researchers, educational administrators and classroom teachers. She describes processes and procedures that dehierarchalise and democratise these relationships and some of the barriers to success in these respects. Her case studies show professionals from different specialisms, not only collaborating for mutual advantage, but also evolving as *communities of learners* who are committed to constructing knowledge about educational change, across the boundaries of their specialist spheres of expertise.

This is her third dimension of learning within the educational change process. She argues that such holistic knowledge is grounded in and tested through action research, into the problems of practice in classrooms and schools.

Many of the case studies in this book reminded me of Lawrence Stenhouse's advice to teachers, when asked by educational theorists to apply their ideas in the classroom. He advised them to instruct the theorists to turn their ideas into a curriculum framework, whose meaning and potential they could investigate within their classrooms. He would approve I think of Keiny's depictions of educational researchers, subject specialists, administrators and teachers learning to construct frameworks for transformative educational action in classrooms and schools together.

Yet in this very respect it can be argued that Keiny goes beyond the image of 'the teacher as a researcher', presented by Stenhouse. Her ecological perspective on educational change provides a more relational and contextualised image of teachers as researchers, that enables her to situate them in multi-professional communities, engaged in constructing knowledge across specialist boundaries. According to this image, teachers are as much shaped by as shaping their interactions with others, in the complex systems they inhabit. Stenhouse's image of 'teachers as researchers' is perhaps rather more 'heroic'; inasmuch as it perhaps stems from a more existential and linear way of thinking, that gives teachers as individuals a great deal of responsibility for determining educational change in their particular contexts of action.

This book will be of interest to all those concerned to conceptualise an alternative paradigm of educational knowledge production, to the one that hierarchically positions itself in relation to educational practice as the definer and arbiter of what counts as good practice. It will enable such readers to appreciate more fully Shoshana Keiny's considerable contribution to this task over the last twenty years.

John Elliott
University of East Anglia. May 2002.

Preface

The roots of my story, which is written in a personal style, as a subjective rather than an objective narrative, are deeply anchored in the Israeli landscape where I was born. A descendant of two pioneer families, both ardent 'Zionists', even before the concept 'Zionism' was coined.

My memories, from as early as I can think, are woven with family history, through stories my grandmother used to tell and retell, and which become an organic part of my own history. Stories about grandpa Hillel "*The Doctor on the Horseback*", being called at the middle of the night to help the young pioneers, who drained the swamps and fell down (like the mosquitoes) with Malaria. Stories about a small community of stubborn people in Palestine, caught in the midst of political struggles between great empires, in World War I. The family history of my father's side, relate the saga of *The Pilgrim Father*, who against all reason left behind the cultural treasures of Victorian England, to settle in the Land of his Fathers.

This heritage or 'family memory' I believe is the source of my notion of a family, as a 'continuity of generation'. A notion that implies an evolutionary perspective, a slower pace as compared to the "process and product" cause-and-effect orientation. In the educational realm, it is reflected in the sense of responsibility we have towards the new generation, coupled with a lack of control over them. I see it is also as the cradle of optimism, of conceiving hard times, even so called catastrophes, as events that have occurred in the past and will also give place to better days. In the same spirit, success is regarded as tentative and temporary, instead of as 'the best solution'.

This family notion implies also a place where one is accepted unconditionally and acts as a person. In our family in particular, you were expected to voice your ideas, open them for discussion, but be prepared to stand for, and live by them. Such a family notion is embedded also in a feeling of respect towards the other and to his/her right to be different, which I believe cannot exist on rationality alone, but requires a basis of affection or love.

Later, as an educator, I adopted the metaphor of a farmer who is 'sowing with the wind', expecting some seeds to germinate in due time, others much later, or maybe not at all. An image so different from the prevailing idea of education as a process of manipulation and control.

Israel as the landscape of my story implies living with change, almost breathing "change": Change of the natural environment from swamps and deserts to a cultivated garden; a change of the human environment as displaced immigrants of different countries became established citizens with full rights. Having the privilege to be born at the time these events take place, I believe I have absorbed the dynamic pace of modern times, as well as the turn of a small and intimate monistic society into a complex multi-ethnic, and pluralistic reality.

The roots of my idea of Ecological Thinking could be traced back to this landscape; ecological thinking as a dialectical relations between the individual and his/her group of reference, a mutuality between the person and his/her community, culture and faith, The implications of this conception to the individual person are enormous: As humans we have the capacity to recreate our world, to reconstruct our society and culture, which on the other hand, constitute the bed of our identity.

My teacher's role perspective, relates back to the days of my 'practical' work, as part of my teacher training studies. As a Biology student teacher, I was required to observe as many classroom activities as possible, mainly in Science. Gaining a wide range of different teachers' performances, it soon became clear to me that many students (if not most) had no idea what the teacher was talking about. Yet, they acquired the 'rules of the game', developing a strategy how to play it. They would use the language, the relevant concepts, the scientific procedures, such as chemical equations, without the faintest idea of what it meant. The extraordinary fact was that the teachers seemed completely unaware of the phenomenon, thereby helping to perpetuate it. In professional terms I can say today, that a majority of the student population acquired a most distorted idea of 'learning', which was not due to any lack of scholastic abilities, but as a result of their schooling.

There and then, I made an oath like promise to myself, never to forget or overlook this gap between the students' overt classroom behavior and their covert actual understanding. I see it as a major educational goal, which might not be fully attained, but serve as a torch whose light guides our action.

A second observation, made somewhat later, concerns the teacher's knowledge. Working with teachers, I came to realize, first intuitively, that they know much more than what they can put into words. Creative classroom performances that seemed to flow almost naturally, could not been explained by their respective teachers. Yet, when questioned, asked to give reason to their methods of coping with unforeseen situations, a rich and deep pool of the teacher's knowledge would emerge, often to the mutual surprise of both researcher and practitioner.

Concepts like reflection, or 'a reflective teacher' were not yet coined. Instead, an awareness, a growing insight has developed to the teacher's tacit knowledge, as a most important vehicle of teaching.

The idea to write this book germinated a decade ago in Cambridge, where I spent a six months' study leave. This beautiful setting that combines one big English garden with the serenity of the traditional English institutes of knowledge, formed an ideal medium for my musing and for self-reflection. I found myself distanced from the tight and over-exciting life at home on the one hand, and on the other, newly exposed to the great polemic debates of that period (of pre and post 1992 elections) over questions of educational values and policy. While dialoguing with my colleagues, I came to construct a new perspective that enabled me to look at my educational experiences through a new set of glasses.

The first version of the book was 'Evaluation of Teachers Professional Development', evaluation being highly resonated in the educational discourse of those days. My proposal was not accepted bt the British publishers, and in the following years my book, rather like a living organism, changed synchronically with its changing context, while maintaining its basic internal organization.

The second version of the book was titled: '*Change as a Challenge for New Thinking in Education*'. Publishers on both sides of the Atlantic, claimed they were saturated with books on 'change', and were not interested to publish anymore on the issue. The other obstacle was more semantic and had to do with the problematic choise of Cybernetics. To define the 'new thinking in education' I used the term: 'second-order Cybernetics'. The turning point was a renewed meeting with my fellow ecologists, a couple of years ago. It was there and then that the modern conception of ecology as an open instead of closed system was introduced. Almost like a flash, all the pieces of the puzzle fell into place: The concept: 'Ecological Thinking' was born, fitting instantly within my conceptual framework.

Shoshana Keiny
Beer-Sheva, June 2002

Acknowledgment

The book is evidently based on many dialogues and conversations, over a long period of time. Some conscious, with friends, colleagues, teachers and students, and others more sub-consciously with 'materials' (in Jeanne Bamberger and Don Schon's words) and mostly with myself. It is hard to distinguish between them, and remember all those who contributed to the process that eventually gave birth to this book.

I shall start with those who are no more with us:

Ben Morris, my first teacher and mentor in Bristol university, who aroused my awareness to the teacher as the main figure in the educational system.

Don Schon, the best listener I was privileged to have, who continuously posed questions, that forced me to probe deeper into the situation.

David Herbst, who created perfect settings for fruitful discussions while 'Walking and Talking' in the beautiful Norwegian landscape, and Tamar Berman's piercing blue eyes, that did not miss a detail.

I am most thankful to the teacher participants, who opened their classrooms, and joined the various reflective groups or communities of learners. Some chose to be mentioned by their real names, and others by pseudonym. I sincerely hope their contribution will be appreciated by all teachers, whom I see as the target population of this book.

Thanks to my good friend and research colleagues, Amos Dreyfus, and to the ardent anthropologist, Hagar Gefen.

Special thanks to my graduate students who helped me crystallize the embryonic half-baked ideas into a conceptual framework.

Thanks to Maya Landau for her sensitive language editing, and to my friend Haim Marantz, for giving the last touches to the completed manuscript.

Finally, to Paulina who relieved me of all the technical aspects of the manuscript, and found elegant solutions to the many problems that kept cropping up, a big garland of thanks.

A last note of apology to my colleagues from the "Desert-Landscape-Seminar", whose extra chapter originally planned to be included in the book, was finally omitted.

Chapter 1

The Conceptual Framework of the Book

In this book, I introduce a new approach to educational change, which I call, 'ecological thinking'. Following Bateson's (Bateson in Harries-Jones, 1995) concept, 'ecological understanding', I relate to ecology as an epistemology, or a way of thinking across different fields such as, engineering, town planning, organizational development, psychotherapy, family life, etc. The underlying assumptions of ecological thinking are self-organization, reflexivity, circular causality, and relationship as the unit of analysis.

The move from closed to open systems in ecology has changed the perceived role of human beings in the system and they are now recognized as important components of systems rather than intruders who disturb the system's equilibrium. As insiders, we *interact* within the system, and as *reflectors*, we are responsible for our own actions and knowledge-constructions.

In this book, I emphasize this double role in educational change. I shall argue that ecological thinking forms the essence of the dialectical learning process that evolves in a 'community of learners', between the individual as an agent within the system and as a reflective actor outside it. To cite Davis and Sumara (1997): "As the learner learns, the context changes simply because one of its components changes. Conversely, as the context changes, so does the very identity of the learner".

Education today subscribes to the possibility of radical educational change. However, the two dominant models for school change – the 'top-down' and 'bottom-up' models – are based on linear thinking. These models imply not only power and control but also cause and effect. This book offers an alternative vision of educational change, one that is built around circular causality, reflexivity, collaboration and interaction – the underlying assumptions of the ecological conception. This approach promotes multidimensional learning of students and teachers as well as of the school as an institution. It entails an alternative conception of teaching and of the role of the teacher.

The starting point of educational change based on ecological thinking is the notion of a 'community of learners'. A community of learners is defined here as a reflective group that recognizes individual differences and freedom of expression of all of its members (Macmurray 1957). Such communities are autonomous and self-organizing, creating their own agendas and assuming responsibility and ownership for their modes of functioning as well as for their 'products' (Herbs 1976).

Communities of learners are also sites for reflection. They create a space for questioning basic assumptions and actions, for dealing with problems and conflicts as they appear in the classroom or at the institutional level, and for participants to take responsibility by experimenting and testing the consequences of their actions. They are places and sites for Action-Research in its various forms, for self-evaluation, curriculum development and professional development.

To illustrate this role of ecological thinking in educational change, I shall draw on the metaphor of a Grandfather Clock. Accordingly, different interacting cogwheels represent the various subsystems that make up the educational system. Thus, the students' cogwheel, rotated by teachers, is also responsible for rotating the teachers' cogwheel (see Chapters 2 and 4). Parents or community members who collaborate with teachers to develop new curricula represent another cogwheel or subsystem in the discourse (see Chapter 3). Other subsystems, such as collaborating researchers or teacher educators, contribute their perspectives as they mutually rotate one another (see Chapters 5, 6, and 7).

In this book, I shall describe the generation of the idea and practice of ecological thinking and how this approach emerged from my collaborative work with teachers. Thus, instead of setting down a cut-and-dried theory, I shall tell the story of a practice and my understanding of that practice. My narrative reflects, my experience with educational change in Israel, a country in which 'change' is a constant phenomenon. It is breathed in with the air – in the transformation of the natural environment from swamps and deserts to a cultivated garden; in the change of the human environment as displaced immigrants from many different countries to become established citizens with full rights and, above all, in cultural change – the rebirth of 2000 year-old tradition and language into a modern way of life.

For sure, educational change is a universal phenomenon and *not* a local issue. The mobility of people across national, cultural and geographic boundaries produces heterogeneous social settings and far-reaching shifts from monocultures to pluralistic multicultural societies the world over. Accordingly, education has become a life-long process involving learning individuals as well as learning organizations; an ongoing process of participation in a discourse rather than mere acquisition of knowledge. Themes such as these form the background of this book.

From Teaching to Learning

The context of practice in this chapter, the 'Science, Technology, Environment and Society' (STES) project, will serve to illustrate the mutual learning process of its participants within a community of learners. The participants in the STES project consisted of teachers from the Environmental Education (EE) High School and researchers from two institutes of research at Sdeh-Boker, a campus of the Ben-Gurion University of the Negev.

For Ben-Gurion (the founding father of the State of Israel), the Negev desert symbolized a major challenge. How to grow food or, indeed, how to survive in the desert, are existential questions that require unique solutions. This challenge faced the Nabbatians who inhabited this region two thousand years ago and it is still relevant today in an era in which the desert is regarded as a scientific, technological, economic as well as a spiritual resource. Thus, the establishment of the Sdeh-Boker campus was both a scientific and a visionary step. Today, it consists of a Scientific Desert Research Institute, highly reputed for its international interdisciplinary research; the Institute for Recent Jewish History Research; and the Unit for Environmental Education, with two affiliated schools: a field school, and an Environmental Education (EE) high school.

The EE high school teachers who participated in the STES project were Hava, a biology and geography teacher, Dan, an English and computer-science teacher, and Oren, a history teacher.   Jointly, they had submitted a proposal for a new integrative curriculum entitled, "Desert and Desertification", which was announced in the internet as a 'Kidlink' project, inviting 'netters', teachers, students, and researchers to join the adventure of learning about the desert and desertification.

The teachers' general concept of the curriculum could be inferred from their proposal. The following excerpt is taken from their 'Notes for the Teachers': "This is not a usual program nor is it a usual curriculum. This is a framework that you, the teacher, will have to fill with relevant subjects... By relevant, we mean here relevance to the student, to the teacher, to the curriculum, or to your environment..."

Collaboration with the other institutes was also mentioned: " We will make contacts with experts from academic institutes who are willing to work with the participants of the project, students and teachers..."

Their long list of educational goals included the following:

- Creating a global and technological learning environment;
- Creating a study environment in which students and teachers will learn from each other;
- Developing an independent student who will be able to generate questions, look for answers, and prepare a report about his/her study;
 - Involving students and making them responsible for the process of learning.

There was no mention in the proposal of the content of the curriculum. The emphasis was on the teacher's role, the teacher's responsibility in formulating the content, and the pedagogical basis of the curriculum.

Their proposal was accepted and they were granted three weekly periods for their new integrative curriculum, in a 10th grade classroom, in the following school year.

Their idea of a learning community, in which teachers and students would learn from one another and where students would develop as autonomous learners, was consistent with my conception of learning. I was particularly attracted to their concept of 'technological environment,' which involved accessing new tracks of information and extending the concept of curricular knowledge.

That is how we came to join forces. Our common target was

to shift away from conventional teacher-centered teaching to student-centered learning.

The literature contains many examples of teachers changing their classroom into a place where students create their own agenda (see, for example, *'The Freedom to Learn'* by Carl Roger). Our aim was to understand the process of change by following it up and ascertaining how we actually learn to make this transition from teaching to learning. We did not believe in applying theories: In our view, educational theories stemmed from practice as a result of practitioners conceptualizing their theories-of-action.

Our approach called for a collaborative rather than a hierarchical context of curriculum change. It meant moving away from the pyramid notion of knowledge construction, which places researchers, as responsible for generating knowledge, at the top, curriculum developers, who translate this knowledge into curricular knowledge, as intermediates, and teachers, who transmit curricular knowledge to students as appliers (as opposed to constructors) of knowledge, at the bottom of the pyramid. Our framework was designed as a collaborative non-hierarchical setting of teachers and researchers working together to create a 'community of learners'.

My suggestion to invite researchers from the two Sdeh-Boker research institutes to join in our project was accepted by the teachers and the school principal, who saw them as assisting in supervising student research studies. Thus, six more participants were recruited: Saar, a desert architect, Moti and Ruth, desert agriculturists from the Desert Research Institute; Orna, a curriculum developer and Avi and Edna, graduate history students, all three from the Jewish History Institute. Aviva, a physics teacher, joined too. Altogether we were four teachers, six researchers, and myself, acting as facilitator. As a collaborative framework, we formed a very heterogeneous group, representing a multidisciplinary scope of knowledge and different modes of inquiry. Each had his or her own reason for joining. However, as we shall see later, we had no idea what this entailed. I believe we were all open to a new adventure and, either as students, lecturers, or parents, we were sensitive to the need to bring about change in the teaching and learning setting. My first aim was to develop the group as a 'community of learners'.

A Community of Learners

The notion of 'community of learners' goes beyond collaboration, per se; it implies collaboration as a means rather than as an end. According to Fielding (1995), collaboration is typified by three dimensions: high-task, low-relationship, and low-equality.   The high-task dimension refers to the fundamentally instrumental motivation for collaboration and its focus on intended gains. The low-relationship dimension refers to participants seeing each other as a source of information or as a resource rather than as a person. This was characteristically expressed, at the beginning of our work as a group, by intolerance to time spent on topics or issues that were not seen as directly connected to the task at hand.   The low-equality dimension was also highly evident in the first stages of our group work, with the teachers tending to look up to the researchers as experts and as a knowledge resource rather than as equal partners. As a result, a within-group hierarchy was evident.

Community is typified by low-task, high-relationship, high-equality and an additional element, high-freedom.   High-relationship and high-freedom facilitate the emergence of a medium in which participants can *be themselves*. Thus, the community becomes a condition for individuality whereby people feel they can voice their 'half-baked' ideas without being ridiculed (Belenky et al. 1986). Reciprocity of freedom and equality implies that roles, positions, status, etc. become latent and do not affect relationship. Indeed, this occurred in our group: Once the researchers came to understand the complexity of the classroom situation, they developed more respect for the teachers and began to relate to them as professionals. The twin commitment to freedom and equality enabled the participants to be exploratory, inventive, and to develop their uniqueness; not as a static state but as an expression of growth and potential, inviting dialogue (Fielding 1995). Belenky uses the term 'real-talk' to define a conversation that included both discourse and exploration typified by talking, listening, questioning, arguing, and speculating. Conversations of this kind trigger reflection and critical thinking. A group reaches this stage only when participants feel safe enough and are able to criticize each other's work and, at the same time, accept criticism. *Thus, the social aspect of the community is reflected in the personal relationship climate that best serves the epistemological goal of the 'community of learners': to reconstruct knowledge.*

The reconstruction of knowledge by the mutual learning of our teachers and researchers was more like a common search of understanding. Neither party, nor I as the facilitator, knew at the outset what outcomes would be reached. Engaging in mutual learning in the sense of "sharing each other's castles" (Somekh 1995) implied mutual respect and equal participation whereby each party tries to understand the other from his or her point of reference. Only at this stage of the discourse can participants feel that they can make new connections that help tie together pockets of knowledge. Belenky describes this as a transition from the 'procedurally connected' to the 'constructivist' way of knowing. No longer subservient to disciplines and systems, participants become responsible for the newly constructed knowledge. (Belenky et al. 1986). This process of learning and of exercising the power of the mind is, indeed, both challenging and exciting.

In summary, our collaborative setting developed into a 'community of learners' through the dialectical process of reflection. As a community of learners, the mutual learning process was enhanced and new understanding was achieved. In other words, new professional knowledge was constructed.

The Framework of the STES Project

The STES project consisted of two interdependent contexts (see Figure 1.1) a social context formed by the community of learners, and a practical context formed by the 10th grade classroom, where the curriculum was practiced. The focus of reflection was the learning experience of the students and the teachers, as well as the joint or mutual learning of the group itself.

A third context of the project was an information-technology medium, namely, the Internet which, by the end of the year, included some 50 teachers and their students from different parts of the world, Internetting with our teachers and their students.

Learning in our community of learners was thus multidimensional or, more precisely, three-dimensional:

The first, basic dimension consisted of the students who had to learn how to initiate a learning process that was of interest and relevance to them. They had to choose their area or topic, formulate a working question, and figure out how to study it.

The second dimension consisted of the teachers who had to learn how to orchestrate a classroom in which students are active learners who initiate their own course of study. Learning on this dimension meant learning how to induce, or to trigger learning. Bateson referred to this dimension as 'second-order learning' in terms of creating new norms, both of classroom teaching and of classroom management.

The third dimension relates to our 'community of learners' consisting of teachers and researchers striving to understand the above learning process. This is the dimension of meta-learning or learning about learning (Bateson in Harries-Jones, 1995).

All group meetings were audio-taped and transcribed, serving for further reflection and as a database for discourse analysis.

The Learning Process

Let us illustrate this three-dimensional learning process by citing excerpts from the collaborative group discourse.

Starting with the second group meeting (9.10.1994), the main issue of the discussion was how to stimulate autonomous learning of students; how to bring them to choose their topic, to ask questions and, at the same time, that is how to 'liberate' them from their customary role of appeasing their teachers or reacting to their implicit cues.

Hava: - We have to start from their reference point. We want to teach them how to ask questions and how to define a topic.... As teachers, we have to think about the kind of pyrotechnics that will stimulate them, such as a list of key words, brainstorming, etc.

Oren: - How do we deal with this new ambiguous situation when we have no idea as to what is going to happen in the next classroom activity. It's both threatening and stimulating.

Saar: - Wider acquaintance with contents would perhaps help them arrive at better questions.

Dan: - Brainstorming could open new possibilities.

This excerpt depicts the very beginning of the group discourse, with participants airing ideas and sharing some of their feelings, anxieties and sense of ambiguity. On the whole, it is a brainstorming situation.

The following excerpt, taken from the third group meeting (16.10.1994), continues along the same track. It relates to events that took place in a recent classroom activity.

Orna: - How can we extend the scope of their choice of topics?

Saar: - Take one question, for example, "the desert in the eyes of contem-porary man" and treat it as an umbrella topic for different sub-questions, questions that emerge from different perspectives of modern times.

Hava: -They keep asking us what is expected of them...

Oren: - We feel as ambiguous as our students.

Moti: - Maybe we are confusing them by putting before them conflicting demands: We ask them to generate ideas from their reference point but, at the same time, we define our requirements for the study.

Figure 1.1: The double locus learning model:

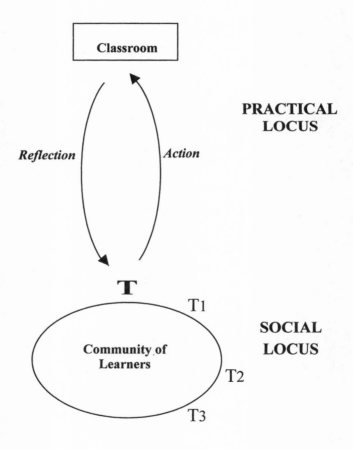

The discourse, which starts as brainstorming, soon moves to a more personal level. The expression of feelings of ambiguity leads to reflection. By questioning our action, Moti triggers the second dimension of learning, namely, awareness of our own modes of action, which may have caused the students' confusion.

The discourse then moves on to deal with different ways of motivating students, for example, by a visit to the Desert Research Institutes.

Dan: - Before planning the visit, we should discuss what we want to achieve? How does it connect with the students' learning?

Orna: - If our aim is to teach them to pursue individual study, I would suggest they meet a researcher and hear directly about his/her current research.

Hava: - I see it differently. The visit should serve as an eye-opener, showing them a wide range of possible topics.

Ruth: - The visit should serve as a kind of concrete experience, as compared to written material.

Dan: - It should open up different sources of knowledge, show them what can be gained from each institute.

Saar: - Instead of exposing them to a wide range of research activities, I would suggest we focus on one issue only and elaborate upon its various aspects and different connected systems. Take, for example, the issue of water recycling: We could show how it is connected to microbiology, to agriculture, to human-systems, etc. This is where I see the 'click' for the student.

This excerpt portrays some second-order learning. The participants do not merely throw out ideas but relate each of them to the learning potential of the visit. Stemming from their different points of reference, it illustrates what I mean by a multi-perspective discourse within a heterogeneous group setting.

Thus, the field visit was seen as having the potential to introduce students to concrete topics of research and extend the range of their choice. It could also focus on methods of research, exposing the students to the way researchers think and how they conduct research. On the practical level, it could facilitate their access to the institutes and, last but not least, it could reveal the interdisciplinary character of research problems.

The visit, which took place shortly thereafter, formed the main topic of the next group discussion. The following excerpt was taken from the fourth group meeting (24.10.1994):

Oren: - The visit was excellent. It opened up a wide scope of interest fields ... for me too... but apart from two students who asked questions, the majority was silent, almost indifferent, as though they were being forced to participate.

Ruth: - They said they were interested yet they seemed tired and passive...

Saar: - Maybe they need to know more in order to be able to ask questions. Alternatively, perhaps we should give them more time for things to sink in.

Orna: - They don't feel secure enough to ask questions.

Edna: - The feedback pages you handed out after the visit may have aroused their antagonism. I think they served to imply that we are back in the old conventional setting, where the teacher controls learning.

All three dimensions of learning are discernible in this short discourse:

On the first basic dimension, contrary to expectation, the students were not aroused; they seemed reluctant, passive, and non-inquiry oriented.

On the second dimension, the teachers realize that they were relating two different messages: On the one hand, they encouraged the students to take responsibility for their learning but, at the same time, they still clung to their old habits of classroom control.

On the third dimension, the group acts as a reflective medium, reflecting on the visit as a concrete learning activity involving both teachers and researchers. Reflection leads to a new understanding of the teachers' role and to the difficulties entailed in making the transition from teaching to learning. Teacher control is now understood in terms of student learning rather than classroom management control.

As a result of the three-dimensional learning process, the original question is rephrased. Instead of "How to stimulate students to become autonomous learners", the new question is: *"How to create a new framework, in terms of classroom norms, that will both encourage as well as allow students to initiate their own learning?"*

This is not merely a repetition of the same question in different words. I see it as a reflection of their new understanding. It indicates a clear shift from general and abstract to more concrete phrasing, as well as a shift of focus from the learners to the teachers. This rephrased question will start a new cycle of questioning of the teachers' style of teaching and open new venues of action and reflection.

What is the significance of this learning? How does it lead to new understanding? All of the participants were experienced and committed teachers, whose frustration with conventional teaching led them to develop the new "Desert and Desertification" curriculum. Ideologically, they believed students should be given the chance to decide what they wanted to learn and the framework to carry out this kind of independent study. Yet, their practice was inconsistent with their 'espoused theories', (Schon 1983) and they were not aware of this. The 'community of learners', acting as a medium for mutual critical reflection, created awareness of this gap. It opened their eyes to seeing the whole of classroom activity in a different way and realizing that the students' reluctance might be connected to their own 'double talk'. Their new vision of the situation led to a new formulation of the problem and the generation of new hypotheses, which could be experimented.

This is what we mean by second-order learning and, in this case, it was mainly teachers' learning, assisted by the researchers. There were other instances where second-order learning was experienced by the researchers. What is pertinent in both cases is that this kind of learning is a painful experience, requiring the collaborative group to act as a 'community of learners'.

My next example of the group's multi-dimensional learning process and their gradual development of understanding relates to the Internet as a basic feature of the project. "How to turn the Internet into a tool of learning" became another issue of discussion. The following excerpts are taken from the 6th group meeting (6.11.1994):

Hava: - The Internet can become another tool in activating students to ask questions. We have several groups of Internetters, from Alaska, from New Zealand, and a group from San Francisco interested in deserts as a context where different faiths developed. Internetting with them could stimulate discussion.

Internetting with other countries is seen as a way of broadening the students' areas of interest and triggering their questions.

Saar: - The students' idea of the desert is rather simplistic, as "a hot place without water" . Internetting with Alaska disclosed the idea of cold deserts, which led to a much wider definition of the desert as "a place where water is inaccessible" .

The Internet is seen here not merely from the multi-perspective view, but as a tool of higher-order learning and deeper understanding; a tool of concept evolution, from the simplistic to the more complex conception.

Moti: - As a result of Internetting, the students will also realize that their conception of the desert as a positive entity, as an ecological system that should not be disturbed, is a very narrow one.

Saar: - We have exposed an ideological debate here: desert and desertification as two contradictory entities.

These excerpts show how the discourse moves from the cognitive level to deeper levels underlying the students' conceptions. For students who chose to study in the Sdeh-Boker EE high school, the desert carries deeply embedded myths, highly resistant to change. In order to escape such 'ideological traps', the issue has to be confronted explicitly.

Avi: - The students are captives of this conception and that is why the visit to the BG Archives cannot liberate their vision...

Orna: - I suggest we encourage them to open these concepts for discussion on the Internet. A variety of responses from different countries and from different points of view could perhaps open their eyes to alternatives, to the multifaceted nature of concepts such as 'desert' and 'desertification'.

Here the Internet is visualized as a tool for open learning situations, where 'netters' are invited to add their different points of view, thus heightening dissonance and loosening our students' fixation.

Implicitly, it could also cope with the problem of motivation, how to motivate them to become active learners. By articulating the deeply embedded ideological conflicts, the students might become stimulated and more involved in the process of their learning.

The issue of the Internet as a learning tool kept coming up in the group discourse yet, it remained tacit. Dan, the computer sciences teacher responsible for the students' internetting experience was constantly struggling with the idea, but only towards the end of the year was he able to articulate his newly generated concept, which he termed "the Internet as a thinking tool".

The following excerpt is taken from the 27th group meeting (21.5.1995):

Dan: - Our plan is to build a clever database that will enable the student to search for an idea or topic, by using keywords which will lead them into smaller data bases. Thus, we create minimized areas of information in an otherwise unlimited resource of knowledge.

Here was a completely novel conception of the use of the internet: as a tool for the students to explore their interest areas within a very open context of knowledge.

The idea was further elaborated at the beginning of the second year of the project. The following excerpt is taken from the first planning session (3.9.1995):

Dan: - A search through the Hypertext is much better adapted to interdisciplinary work, more adapted to opening up ideas. In a library search, the books are already catalogued on the basis of organizing topics. The whole point of the Internet is that it is not classified. The student interacts directly and, in this way, develops his or her thinking. We will have to organize the data pool accordingly and let the student learn by his own experience – a database based on a menu system that will navigate the beginner student, after which, the 'sky is the limit'.

I chose this example to illustrate the interplay between theory and practice in the group learning process. In Dan's case, the practice takes place in the world of computers and, in particular, the Internet. He begins with a vague idea of developing it as a learning tool and, intuitively, puts the idea into practice. Now the classroom becomes an experiential setting for him and the other teachers to reflect upon and conceptualize the practice into a broader understanding. Gradually, the Internet is seen not merely as a tool for collecting additional information, or accessing different perspectives and achieving higher-order learning, but as a tool in the search for ideas or topics. (The image I see in my mind is that of a wanderer in an open landscape, searching for something that will attract his or her interest). Dan sees the Internet as serving two functions simultaneously: A tool for the student to learn how to conduct a search for ideas, and a database to develop a hypertext consisting of different contexts of knowledge for the student to wander about and choose his or her venue.

This second example again illustrates our three-dimensional learning: On the second dimension, starting from the question, "What do we mean by learning from internetting?" the teachers try internetting as part of their classroom activity and reflect on its various potentials as an aid to increasing the scope and depth of our understanding and conceptual development.

On the first dimension, the students learn how to use this tool more effectively, which makes them more comfortable with it. By the end of the year, they complete their research studies, adding them to the database, which then grows in content and in multi-perspectiveness. This then becomes the basis for the teachers to enrich the construction of the hypertext.

On the third dimension, the group's focal question was how to handle all this information. This is a variation on the question, "How do we create a new framework for learning?" Both deal with the interface between ordered and open situations, such as learning with no teacher control, or searching in an unstructured context of information. This is what we mean by meta-learning, learning how to think and how to search in authentic situations (which, by definition, are of an interdisciplinary rather than disciplinary nature). I regard these as important steps towards new thinking – towards conceptual change.

Conceptual Change

A number of theories of conceptual change (CC) have been offered in the area of education (see, for example, Duit 1994, Steffe and Gale 1995). The "Initial Conceptual Change" theory (Posner et al. 1982), developed by science educators and philosophers of science, is a cognitive model based on Piaget, Kuhn, Lakatos, Toulmin, and others. An alternative theory of conceptual change, introduced by the Swedish phenomenographic school, challenges the purely cognitive perspective, suggesting instead an experientially based model (Linder 1993, Marton 1986).

Our thinking is more in line with the latter approach in that rather than viewing conceptual change from a cognitive perspective, we see it as *'a change in the person's relationship with the world'* (Marton and Booth 1997, Gorodetsky and Keiny 2002). Conceptual change is somewhat like paradigmatic change in that it involves a new way of seeing or understanding the world. In Albert Einstein's words, "We cannot solve the problems that we have created, with the same thinking that created them", which I chose as the motto of this book, alludes to this notion of 'new thinking'. Indeed, a paradigmatic shift in our understanding of reality is a pre-requisite for new educational thinking and practice.

To explain what I mean by this paradigmatic shift or conceptual change, I shall try to juxtapose the two conceptions, the positivistic versus the ecological, by confronting each with the following three questions:

The ontological question: What is the nature of the world of reality?

The epistemological question: What is the nature of knowledge?

The ethical question: What is the nature of man or of society? (Aviram et al. 1992).

Comparison of the two conceptions, the positivistic and the ecological along the above three perspectives will illustrate my meaning.

   a) *Ontologically*, according to the positivistic conception, the world, which consists of objects, events, and processes, exists independently of human perceptions, thoughts or theories. The phenomena of nature are manifestations of the rules of nature. It is the role of the scientist to reveal these rules. In this sense, scientific theories are discovered.
   According to the ecological conception, 'reality' is a function of human subjective perception and experience, because there is no other access to the world 'out there.' To cite Glasersfeld:

> Since Kant and Hume it is clear that we have no access to reality. The only way is to construct our own interpretations, own realities, and adapt these subjective constructs through trial and social interaction until they function with sufficient success. We can arrive at viable (feasible, existing) solutions and models only, which are formed until further notice. There is never any reason to believe that this construction is the only one possible... (Glasersfeld 1987)

In other words, scientific theories are *invented and not discovered* and, as such, there is no one 'correct' representation of the world. 'Reality' is the total sum of all the different conceptions of reality of participants in a particular context.

   b) *Epistemologically*, knowledge, according to the positivists, is an external objective entity, consisting of structured bodies of knowledge termed disciplines. Each has a distinct boundary, created by its specific concepts and methodology (Schwab 1964).

According to the ecological conception, knowledge, being an individual subjective construction, is subjective. We each construct our idiosyncratic concepts, which, through social interaction, language, and discourse, 'fit' but never completely 'match' (Glasersfeld 1989). Thus, it follows that there is no one truth. Knowledge is Rashumon like in that it is multifaceted. Scientific knowledge is that knowledge which the scientific community has accepted as the best interpretation of the world, leaving open edges for new theories that will offer a wider explanatory power (Kuhn 1962).

c) *Ethically,* the positivistic conception of society is hierarchical, distinguishing between different professional groups, between experts and non-experts. There is a distinct division between theory and practice, between researchers as knowledge constructors and practitioners as knowledge appliers. Thus, in terms of knowledge construction, the researchers are located at the top of the pyramid and the teachers, as 'users' or knowledge transmitters, are located at the bottom (Keiny 1987).

In contrast, the ecological main principle is 'interaction,' in the sense of interdependence and inter-relatedness between the different components of the world, both in the natural context (as between organisms and inanimate matter, between people and the biosphere, etc.) and the social context. This implies a more democratic and less hierarchical orientation of social interaction and collaboration, a society based on mutual respect and the right to be different.

This kind of interaction was termed by cyberneticians as 'first-order cybernetics'. 'Second-order cybernetics' refers to the relationship between a person as an observer and his or her reality as a subject of study (Maturana 1992). The human individual is both an actor and a reflector of his or her actions (Macmurray 1957). According to Foerster, this implies taking responsibility for one's observations and interpretations of the world; taking responsibility for one's system of knowledge and personal conception (Foerster 1992, Maturana 1992). This double role of an insider as an actor within the system and as an outside reflector who is aware of and responsible for his or her knowledge and action, is what we mean by 'Ecological Thinking' (ET), a term interchangeable with 'second-order cybernetics'.

Thus, compared to the positivistic values of objectivity and neutrality, the ecological conception of society is more egalitarian and collaborative. The values to which it aspires include personal responsibility, involvement, and commitment.

Let us return to my story. The full meaning of the STES project can now be realized. Its rationale was based on the ecological paradigm, whereby students are expected to understand the world, including the natural, technical and social phenomena around them, to become aware of the impact created on their lives by our society and culture, and to take responsibility in dealing with authentic problems in order to bring about change. However, as already mentioned, although ideologically accepted by our participants (those who disagreed did not take part in the project), there was a gap between this ideology as an espoused theory and the participants' grounded theories; their theories-in-action (Schon 1983). Conceptually, they were stuck somewhere between positivism and ecological thinking. The STES framework, was planned to create an optimal medium for enhancing the process of their conceptual change.

Based on the interactive double locus model, (see Figure 1.1) the STES project consists of two loci, the locus of practice and the social locus. The teacher (T) in the model is exposed to both. The teachers' main field of practice is the classroom, where he or she acts as an individual and by reflecting *on* or *in* action, the teacher constructs and reconstructs his/her practical knowledge.

The social context is the reflective group (in our case, the 'community of learners'), where teachers exchange ideas with their colleagues and engage in a dialectical process of reflection, constructing and reconstructing professional knowledge (Keiny and Dreyfus 1989). However, unless this new understanding is translated into action and is experimented in the classroom, it remains a theoretical idea, and the group's learning is no more than an intellectual exercise. The classroom as the teacher's practical context is where the new ideas can be tried, reflected upon, and judged in relation to both their intended goals and to the participant's deeper beliefs and basic assumptions.

There is no necessary sequence between the two contexts, the practical context can precede the social context, and vice versa. Our emphasis is upon their mutuality or interdependence.

The model represents also the promotion of two types of knowledge construction: The teacher's practical knowledge constructed and reconstructed by the individual teacher in the classroom, and a more formal type of professional knowledge, constructed through critical reflection within the group context (Fenstermacher 1994).

Another way of looking at this interplay is through the debate between the two constructivist theories of learning, the radical and the sociocultural, as to the locus of knowledge construction. "Does the construction of knowledge occur in the person's mind or in the individual-in-social-action?" (Cobb 1994) Like Cobb, we contend that these two perspectives of constructivism are complementary, congruent with our notion of learning as an interactive process, where "the cognizant individual can test the viability of his or her constructed knowledge only by interacting with other members of the community" (Glasersfeld 1992).

Evaluation of the STES Curriculum

From the very start of our group work, the teachers found themselves struggling with the issue of evaluation or, more specifically, with the question of how to assess their students' learning. The following three principles were finally articulated:

- Assessment of students' final research studies will indicate the extent of their conceptual change from positivism to ecological thinking.
- New methods based on new criteria of evaluation will have to be established;
- These criteria can be used for evaluation of our new curriculum unit "Desert and Desertification".

As I ran through the transcripts of the group discourse, I realized that my efforts to introduce some theoretical background on evaluation as a trigger for elaboration had not taken root. I felt that my words were understood and well appreciated but they were not applied in practice and, as such, remained 'outside' ideas. It became clear to me that the notion of evaluation had to stem from the actual *practice of evaluation* within the group.

The opportunity for this was provided by the students' final assignments, which were submitted at the end of the school year. These assignments portrayed a wide scope of topics and styles, that ranged from a scientific format to an imaginative description of an encounter with a monk in the desert. They had to be assessed and marked by the teachers for the final certificates. The group decided to involve all members in the process. We all read the students' research reports in order to extract our criteria of evaluation.

I have chosen a few excerpts from the 25th and 26th group meetings (7.5.1995, 14.5.1995) to illustrate how our criteria of evaluation emerged from the students' assignments.

Dan: - (goes through the titles of his students' studies):
-   -The geology of Eilat - including computer-made drawings;
    - Penguins in the cold desert;
    - Migration of birds in the desert
    - The Nabbatian culture;
    - Some uses of plants - in collaboration with Arizona;
    - Groundwater - in comparison with Alaska;
    - Desert sculpture in relation to the landscape;
    - A comparison between Eskimo and Massai nomads.

The group discourse that follows dwells on the wide range of subjects, as well as on the impact made by internetting (with Arizona or Alaska) on the students' choice of study.
From the general level, the discussion moved to a more particular level:

Oren: - I have some problems. Take, for example, Shai's work on the migration of birds. It is based on his daily observations, as well as his own drawings. There is no doubt about the high quality of his fieldwork. However, there is a complete lack of some kind of theoretical background to compare his findings with the work of others. Another thing I thought was lacking was some meaningful personal conclusions.

Oren's comment implicitly points to two criteria of evaluation: the interaction or confrontation of different forms of knowledge (theoretical and empirical), and the voicing of personal thoughts, or the 'personal voice' of the student.

Oren: - (continues) Another study submitted by a pair of excellent field people contains an extensive survey of desert flora. A very serious piece of work, but purely disciplinary, no element of interdisciplinarity.

'Interdisciplinarity' is another criterion characterizing the new conception.

Moti: - I see these assignments as part and parcel of our own self-evaluation process, of what we intended to develop here. As 'products' of learning, they could also serve as data for evaluating *our* work.

Saar: - The bottleneck was the teachers' process of learning and under-standing. Take the case of Shir. Her work clearly indicates our reluctance to interfere with the students' own choice of questions... We shall have to learn how to navigate them without directing them.

The two last comments, which reflect on our own group work, convey the feeling of joint responsibility. The students' research studies are seen as indicators of the extent of *our* learning and new understanding, which becomes the limiting factor. As a group, it is our responsibility to find a way. This, to me, reflects the mutuality of the three-dimensional learning process. I shall return to this point later.

Aviva: - Shir happens to be a highly intelligent girl. She decided to play it small and chose to investigate "the flooding of the Revivim river and its effect on the region", an issue well covered in the research literature. She has a natural fluency but altogether, it is a typical theoretical assignment, the kind we wanted to avoid. There is no single original idea; nothing of her own voice.

The students' personal interaction with the material is a fourth criterion; that is, taking responsibility for the newly constructed knowledge, the main principle of ecological thinking.

These short excerpts were chosen to illustrate how the group discussion and critical reflection, on the products of our joint curriculum development, actually helped highlight the criteria that characterize the new curriculum.

The next step was to juxtapose these criteria with the STES rationale. The following principles were obtained:

Multidisciplinarity, or multifacetedness, different aspects of the topic;

Interdisciplinarity, the interaction between these different aspects, between different forms of knowledge to yield a newly constructed knowledge, or creative new thinking;

Personal involvement, the student's own voice, based on his or her values and belief system.

By comparison with previous studies (Gorodetsky and Keiny 1996), we were able to validate each of these principles or dimensions. Moreover, an additional dimension was disclosed, namely, *Dynamism,* reflecting the ability to conceive reality as an ever-changing process on the axis of time. Dynamism signifies the *process* of change, which, in our curriculum unit, was represented by 'desertification', as opposed to the more static concept of 'desert'.

This finding was consistent with our impression of the complete neglect of 'desertification'. None of the students' research studies alluded to desertification or to the concept of change. I decided to trace our discourse on 'desertification' in the 22nd group meeting (two months before the students' studies were evaluated):

Moti: - I am concerned with the fact that their projects do not relate to the time dimension; they convey the 'here and now'. I am disturbed by the fact that they are stuck in the classical static orientation and do not take the dynamics of change into account.

That is why I am keen to develop 'desertification' as a key concept. As a dynamic concept, it could stimulate questions such as: "Is desertification a negative or positive process?" "Is it a natural cyclic process?"   "How does external interference such as provision of food and medication, inhibit natural processes?".

This excerpt serves to illustrate our sensitivity as a group to the students' lack of dynamism, or grasp of the dynamics of change. Based on the assumption that by dealing with the issue from the moral aspect of intervention and change we could still create the necessary impact on the students' learning, a number of practical steps were implemented.   It should be emphasized that desertification was seen as a metaphor, a metaphor for the process of change (positive and negative) caused by the intervention of humankind in nature.

To sum up, our evaluative activity served two purposes. The immediate, explicit purpose was to assess the students' work as indication of their learning process. The more implicit purpose was to evaluate the new integrated curriculum; its internal coherence as reflected by the congruence between the manifested rationale and the learning activity. It was particularly important to examine the extent to which it was congruent with the new ecological paradigm. In this respect, we were actually evaluating our own learning and conceptual change.

Educational Change

The focus of this book is the notion of change – the need to change our way of perceiving reality, of relating to our world, and of practicing education.   My main argument is that the massive social changes that have taken place over the past 50 years, and which have affected almost every aspect of our lives (such as, work patterns, residential stability, sexual habits, dress, language, music, etc.) have not been matched by new thinking in education.

The global market economy has become the paradigm not only for economic policy but also for public institutions (Waks 1995). Schools are urged to think of themselves as business organizations with economic value being assigned only to marketable products. Concepts from the marketplace, such as productivity, efficiency, competition, and re-engineering have replaced the more human discourse about ethics and responsibility. Accordingly, curriculum changes have been mainly technological, such as the introduction of computerized learning activities, or the 'virtual classroom'. Whether these devices improve the learning process or not seems to be secondary. The dominant message they carry is that people, in this case, teachers, can be replaced by technology. It seems that 'technological thinking' has replaced 'educational thinking' in dictating our educational discourse.

I believe the time has come to move away from 'production models' and to start thinking in terms of 'growth models'. In Ursulla Franklin's words: "If there ever was a growth process, that cannot be divided into rigid predetermined steps, it is education" (Franklin 1991).

My paradigm of new thinking in education involves a different approach to the basic questions in education grounded in a new perception of the world and a new conception of reality. The basic assumption of this new paradigm is the inseparability of theory from practice or, in Aristotelian terms, educational knowledge as *phronesis*, as practical wisdom. Phronesis constitutes *insight* acquired through a process of reflection upon, and judgment of personal experience, which, in turn, leads to choice of action and confrontation with its consequences (Kessels and Korthagen 1996).

This is precisely the reason for choosing this style of writing, that is, presenting my story of the learning process in which we, the participants, conceptualized our educational practice. My case study, based on the work of our collaborative group of teachers and researchers, jointly developing a new curriculum, is an illustration of multidimensional learning. Multidimensional, in this context, means a mutual process of learning, one that involves students, teachers learning to orchestrate this type of learning in the classroom, and the group's meta-learning of the nature of this learning, that is, professional knowledge. A necessary prerequisite for the process of multidi-mensional learning was the development of a 'community of learners' as the optimal context for new knowledge reconstruction or new understanding; a framework for the participants' (teachers, researchers, students, parents, etc.) conceptual change.

Before winding up this part of my story, one more question needs to be addressed, namely, "How does this new thinking enhance systemic educational change?"

Most educational initiatives towards change, whether by the top-down algorithm model or the bottom-up action research model, involve linear thinking. Top-down intervention, in most cases, forces teachers to act like small cogs in a machine. Their responsibility is to apply and carry out innovative ideas generated by external 'others', who are assumed to be experts in the field. This strengthens their instrumental role or instrumental position in the system and, as such, they are constantly blamed by the system as well as by educational researchers for their lack of initiative and creative thinking (Lorti 1975).

The alternative movement of 'school self-renewal' or 'action research in the classroom' involves a bottom-up perspective of change. Assuming that "the school is the teachers" and that "teachers form the resource pool needed for change", it is they who are seen as the best 'sensors' of the system and of their students' needs and, as such, they are the ones to initiate change (Schmuck et al. 1975). However, this bottom-up movement, which often succeeds in bringing about classroom or even school change, has failed to gain the critical mass necessary for a more comprehensive, larger systemic change. Thus, formal educational systems in most western countries tend to adhere to old agendas. As a result, we find the teachers torn between their genuine desire to change and the demands of the conservative establishment of educational policy.

The linear thinking of these two paradigms of school change implies not only power and control but also cause and effect. The concept of educational change offered here is at once *circular, interactive and non-hierarchical,* and based on *collaboration and mutual multidimensional learning.* To illustrate this new concept, I shall use the metaphor of the 'Grandfather Clock'.

The Grandfather Clock

Unlike the conventional clock, the mechanism of the grandfather clock is exposed, revealing a system of interlocking cogwheels, which indicate 'the time' or 'the passing of time'. The educational system can be seen as a grandfather clock in which the cogwheels stand for the different subsystems, such as teachers, researchers, students, etc. The main subsystem is that of the students, who are the subjects, the core of the whole system. The student subsystem (cogwheel) is rotated by the second most important cogwheel, that of the teachers. At the same time, the student cogwheel also rotates the teachers' cogwheel.

For example, in the STES project, it was shown that the teachers promoted their students' learning, guiding them in their research process. At the same time the students' independent studies promoted teachers' learning, their reflection and reconstruction of professional knowledge.   Moreover, the students' assignments led their teachers to change their previous assumptions about teaching and learning as well as their beliefs about students' inability to act as autonomous learners. This is what I mean by a process of mutual learning.

The researchers constitute the third cogwheel.   Their interaction with the teachers, can also be seen as mutually rotating one another. The dialectical tension between the researchers' formal knowledge, their more formal mode of inquiry, and the teachers' practical knowledge or more practical mode of inquiry, enhanced the mutual learning process in the group (Fenstermacher 1994). This idea will be further elaborated in Chapter 6 of this book.

To achieve educational change, more cogwheels or subsystems have to be drawn into the process, such as that of the parents or other members of the community. Parents today are inclined to be more involved in their children education. However, as members of the community, they voice its socio-cultural ideas, including its 'cultural myths'.   This may explain the tension between teachers and parents with regard to innovation in the school.   Indeed, that is why they should be drawn into the discourse and participate in the process of learning and gaining new understanding of education.

Examples of collaborative teams consisting of teachers and parents, as well as other community representatives, who worked jointly to turn their school into a 'community school', are presented in Chapter 5 of this book. Drawing parents into the educational discourse and treating them as partners improves the chance of turning them into advocates of school change and providing their children more (rather than fewer) educational opportunities.

An important missing 'cogwheel' is that of the administrators and policy makers. They too should be drawn into the discourse to ensure the translation of the new ideas and new understanding into structural changes that can be applied in practice. Slogans such as autonomous-learning, critical-thinking, team-teaching, school-based-curriculum-development, and many others, have become part and parcel of the educational discourse. Yet, in order for these concepts to be translated into actual educational practice, they have to become important issues on the educational agenda.

Our collaborative framework of mutual learning is an example of a '*polytextual discourse*' between the different parties or subsystems, a polytextual discourse that has the capacity to bring about educational change.

I roundup my story with a quote from Maturana:

> And since we exist in language, the domain of discourse that we generate becomes part of our domain of existence, constituting part of the environment in which we conserve identity and adaptation. Language was never invented by anyone only to take in an outside world. Therefore it cannot be used as a tool to reveal the world. Rather it is by languiging that the act of knowing brings forth the world. (1980)

Chapter 2

Action-Research in the School

This chapter is based on two Action-Research (AR) projects. Retrospectively, the first project can be seen as pilot for the second project.

In my recently completed Ph D thesis, I advocated a new approach to teacher training aimed at enhancing the 'developmental' as opposed to the 'instrumental' role of teachers. The research population, which consisted of three cohorts of student teachers, participated in an experiential course based on T-group methods. A significant conceptual change in their role was observed, from that of teachers as knowledge transmitters (the intstrumental role), to that of developmental teachers responsible for cultivating active learners. The opportunity to try out my newly constructed ideas in the field presented itself when a large comprehensive school in my hometown invited me to act as an external consultant.

The Israeli comprehensive school is based on the British model introduced by Labor governments after World War II, in an attempt to promote 'equal opportunity in education'. The non-selective comprehensive schools, designed for all secondary school students living in a particular catchment area, are large institutions accommodating a variety of curricular learning tracks. Israel had her own reasons for adopting the comprehensive school model. The establishment of the State of Israel in 1948 was followed by massive waves of immigration from western as well as eastern countries. 'Social integration' was the motto of the day, and the comprehensive school was seen as a kind of 'melting-pot'. It offered a venue for a wide range of educational tracks, hence catering for both academic and vocational students, depending on inclination and aptitude. The phenomenon of 'creaming off' or the tendency for bright students to enroll at more prestigious selective schools was avoided because, in the newly developing regions of Israel (especially in the south), comprehensive schools were the only form of secondary education available. Personally, as a young teacher at a comprehensive school, I was caught up by the new challenge. It meant searching continuously for new methods of teaching and having to deal with a heterogeneous population of students in terms of their ethnic and socio-economic background as well as their learning abilities.

In those early days, 'resistance to change' was a much-quoted concept (by Schmuck, Miles, Liberman, Goodlad and others). It was thus heartening to find a school principal eager to collaborate with an outsider. For me, this was an indication that she was open, rather than resistant to change. After succeeding in capturing the interest of two of my colleagues, the three of us plunged into the project. None of us were acquainted with the term, 'Action-Research'. We decided to take an experiential stance to whatever was meant by 'school resistance' and study the practice of implementing our project. Intuitively, we felt that by working 'on the inside', we would be in a position to gain better an understanding of, and insight into, the phenomenon of school resistance to change, on the one hand, and school self-renewal, on the other.

School Self-Renewal

It is generally accepted that schools should renew themselves or, at least, that the staff should be able to deal creatively with problems in the school. In other words, they should define problems, search for solutions, test them and, accordingly, reach operational conclusions. This decision-making and problem-solving process forms the central feature of the various self-renewal models described in the literature (e.g., Schmuck, Murray, Schwartz and Runkel 1975, French and Bell 1973, Fullan, Miles and Taylor 1980). However, in general, schools do not adapt themselves easily to the demands of self-renewal programs.

In my view, the difficulties in implementing self-renewal methods stem from the fact that they are generally developed by outside experts and then imposed upon the teachers instead of being based upon the teachers' own theories-in-action (Schon 1983). Recent studies show that teachers possess their own theories about what they do and what is reasonable, feasible and possible in the classroom. Their 'teaching knowledge' is based on living experience rather than on the wisdom of outside experts (Smith 1984, Shulman 1987).

In contrast, educational action-research is a form of reflective inquiry undertaken by participants with the aim of improving the rationality and justice of their own educational practice, their own understanding of the practice, and the contexts in which this practice is carried out (Carr and Kemmis 1983). The term 'educational action-research' is used to refer to a whole set of activities such as curriculum development, professional development as well as school improvement. It is concerned with four identified strategies of planned action: the practical *implementation* of the teacher's task, which is systematically submitted to *observation; reflection* – making the teacher aware of the situation, and the need to be prepared to *change* should he or she believe this to be necessary. Though often undertaken by individuals, action-research is most effective when exercised in groups in collaboration with 'outsiders'. Thus, the introduction of the action-research approach meant involving teachers in collaborative curricular projects as internal researchers (Stenhouse 1982).

Typical of many similar initiatives, the desire for change had triggered the school to act even before the goals of such action had been defined. As a result, no real change had been achieved and, as already mentioned, we were called in to help handle the process initiated by the school. Our first task was to recruit and train team leaders from among the school's teacher-volunteers. The next phase was to divide the school staff into teams (five in all) based on teachers' choice of topic or team leader. Once formed, the teams met regularly once a fortnight for the rest of the school year. The team leader group –intensively supervised by us, the external consultants – also met regularly. Our aim was to develop them as experienced 'internal consultants' (Miles and Fullan 1980).

The following topics were chosen for the group work of the five teams:
(1) Improving the quality of life in school.
(2) Improving the professional ethics of teachers.
(3) Improving teacher-student relations.
(4) Improving teaching methods in low-ability classes.
(5) Increasing parent involvement in the school.

Our research team consisted of three researchers (or consultants) and two research students whose task was to record and transcribe all of the team meetings. They were also responsible for all other data collection, such as interviewing a sample of participant teachers and gathering feedback from students.

Though not explicitly formulated, our rationale was based on the following basic assumptions:

(1) The school is its teachers.
(2) The teachers, more than any other party, sense the school's problems and its areas of malfunction.
(3) Teachers have the potential resources for changing and renewing the school but this potential is not fully realized.
(4) It is the role of the 'outsider' to identify these resources.
(5) Becoming aware of these resources is coextensive with the processes of personal growth.
(6) Personal growth is coupled with institutional growth (Schmuck 1975).

These assumptions reflect a developmental rather than instrumental perception of the teacher's role and the teaching profession. Accordingly, generalizations derived from past experiences cannot be formulated to provide general rules prescribing good practice. However, as *retrospective* generalizations, they may be of help to the teacher as sensitizers, facilitating the development of new insight in redefining the situation (Stenhouse 1975). Thus, retrospective generalizations may orient the teacher to formulate his or her own theory-in-action (Schon 1983). In this sense, the developmental teacher is a *generator* of professional knowledge rather than an *applier* of knowledge formulated by educational theorists (Stenhouse 1975, Ebbutt and Elliott 1983).

In the following, I relate the story of our intervention as inside-researchers. To illustrate the process of learning and development in the teams, I chose to follow the progress of a team whose topic was to improve teaching methods in low-ability classrooms.

The Process

Low-ability classes are generally populated by culturally disadvantaged students. However, the aim of the team was not to find out why but rather who they were and how to teach them effectively. They decided to gather knowledge about these students in order to arrive at a better understanding of their learning difficulties. How to gain access to a wide range of information was the opening question for discussion. It was a large and hetereogenous group, and they could each choose their preferred mode of data collection. Thus, the theoretically inclined members chose to further their knowledge by reading from books and journals dealing with the issue. The active types chose to gather information from the field by interviewing teachers, students, etc. The impatient 'doers' tried experimenting in their own classes and observing their colleagues' teaching activities. This form of simultaneous data gathering involving differently motivated teachers has been described in more detail. (see Keiny et al. 1987, Dreyfus, Keiny and Kushnir 1989)

As a result, a great deal of information, both practical and theoretical was gathered and consequently reported in the team meetings.   The confrontation between theory and practice, between reflective observation and active experience, created a dialectical tension (Kolb and Fry 1975), which heightened the teachers' awareness. They were better able to see the problem within its context, and *to realize that they were part of it*. They soon realized that their feelings of frustration were caused by their failure as teachers in the low-ability classes.   Moreover, they became aware to the fact that instead of dealing with these problems, they tended to blame the students for being stupid and unmanageable. These defense mechanisms on the part of the teachers resulted in parallel mechanisms on the part of the students, namely, indifference, lack of motivation and alienation. Thus, instead of helping the students, the increasing gap between them and the teachers only intensified their learning difficulties and, at the same time, emphasized the teachers' failure to reach the students, and so on, in a vicious circle.

We regard the stage of *diagnosing the hidden underlying problem* as an essential step in the process, and a prerequisite for further handling of the problem. We believe it is comparable with what Bateson (1972) termed 'deutero-learning or second-order change' (Watzlawick et al. 1974).

It is possible now to distinguish between the symptoms and the basic problem.   By symptoms, I mean the things that immediately strike us as being wrong; in our case, the outward signs of dissatisfaction sensed by the teachers.   The 'basic problem' is the hidden reason for, or cause of the symptoms, yet to be diagnosed.

I believe that many change programs have failed because of their tendency to deal only with symptoms. By creating a first-order change, or 'more-of-the-same', they achieve perpetuation rather than a change of the system (Watzlawick et al. 1972). The work of another team will serve to illustrate the distinction between symptoms and basic problems.

The team dealing with the quality of life at school consisted of a dominant group of highly experienced teachers and a young team leader. They began their work by trying to characterize what they meant by poor quality of life in the school. Their identified symptoms included noise, rowdiness, disorder, unattractive physical appearance, etc. Impatient to introduce change, the team never stopped to wonder why the norms of behavior of students (and teachers, for that matter) in the school were different from those adhered to in the home. Instead of trying to extend their pool of knowledge in order to diagnose the underlying basic problem, they jumped into action: cleaning, decorating, pot-planting, etc., dealing with the symptoms in a-more-of-the-same way. The consequences were no different from similar initiatives in the past, hence justifying the saying, 'the more things change, the more they stay the same'(Sarason 1971).

In contrast, the teachers of the team working on improvement of teaching methods in low-ability classrooms, were quick to recognize that they had become entrapped in a vicious circle. This recognition, in itself, had a powerful impact and led to their changing their perceptions of the situation. Liberated from their one-track thinking, they were now able to use their new insight and redefine the situation.

Although the team did not succeed in defining any practical solutions during the first year, as a result of their personal change, its members arrived at higher awareness regarding their intitution's inadequacy in handling the low-ability classes and culturally disadvantaged students. Consequently, the school management was able to reflect on the logic of their policy; their declared norms: The comprehensive school policy was to equalize the teaching effort throughout the school so as not to crowd the 'good classes' with 'good teachers'. As a result, teachers who were unprepared and unmotivated to teach low-ability students tended to be assigned to these classes. Thus, instead of enhancing equality of opportunity, they came to realize that this practice actually intensified the gap, making it a typical case of what Sarason (1971) described as a secondary problem developing from the mishandling of the original problem.

The school's management enhanced awareness of the situation resulted in a number of new decisions: It was decided that the teaching staff in the low-ability classes would be comprised only of teachers who *chose* and, therefore, were *motivated* to teach such students. Secondly, the teaching staff of each of these classes would form a team and hold regular weekly meetings. Functioning rather like a workshop, both educational and learning issues would be discussed at these meetings. The home-teacher or the school counselor would act as team leader. These decisions were to be carried out as institutional changes in the following school year.

The Second Year

Three teams, each consisting of the full teaching staff of three low-ability classes were formed. The proceedings of their weekly morning sessions were recorded, transcribed, and circulated among the participants. The team leaders' group, which was supervised by the external consultant, met regularly twice a month. Having had no previous training, the team leaders had to learn their role while in action.

In one of their early sessions, the team leaders' group decided on a common problem to be tackled in the individual teams, namely, "How to change the students' general feeling of antagonism towards the school and, thereby (hopefully), improve their functioning".

This was a difficult problem. In the meantime, in the weekly sessions, a clear consistent policy of action was agreed upon by the participants and their collaborative treatment of common issues yielded quick success. For example, a consistent policy for dealing with student absentees and latecomers reduced their number to a minimum. Common awareness of the neglected appearance of classrooms (disorder, broken chairs, bare walls, etc.) led to their quick transformation into more attractive, orderly learning places. Similarly, the collaborative treatment of the students' style and tone of speech significantly improved class communication as well as relations among students and between teachers and students. To cite some of the teachers' observations:

- You can hardly recognize the class...
- It's a pleasure to teach them now.
- It's fantastic to see how they have learned to listen to one another...

These quick changes increased the teachers' motivation for further involvement in their teamwork. After the removal of overt factors such as inconsistent learning, poor communication, prejudiced and low-motivated teachers, a more fundamental problem surfaced: *"How to initiate significant learning in these classes"*. The team decided on a new route of action with the aim of improving student learning.

The following excerpt taken from a team session dealing with individual cases will illustrate their teamwork:

Team leader: - (the home-teacher, reporting on a problem case), ...They nickname him 'mechanics' because this is the only subject he attends.

Mechanics teacher: - He is very good. I was surprised to hear from the students that this is the one and only lesson in which he participates. (His words provoke general surprise.)

Team leader: - (moving on to another boy), And what do you have to say about Yigal?

Mechanics teacher: - Excellent! Likes to work. Stays on overtime. (Again this provokes surprise.)

Team leader: - What about his behavior?

Mechanics teacher: - Good enough. A bit uneven, but he does what he is told.

English teacher: - That just shows how important these sessions are. Before you came, we drew such a negative picture of Yigal. I realize now it was only half the picture...

Team leader: - ...all that could be said about him is that he is childish, extro-verted.

Mechanics teacher: - He is very childish.

Team leader: - (continuing), ...that he doesn't work and misbehaves. The biology teacher claims that there isn't one positive thing about him except that he surely has potential. We are keen to understand how it is that he is so good in your subject. What triggers him?

Mechanics teacher: - He even helps the others.

Music teacher: - It may have to do with the fact that we are the only men on the teaching staff.

Team leader: - We are not referring to discipline problems.

Mechanics teacher: - It may be because of the subjects I teach. They interest him, and they don't demand too much effort. Some of the theoretical subjects are above the students' heads.

Team leader: - You are talking about two different things.

Mechanics teacher: - He doesn't create any discipline problems. The only difficulty arises once he finishes his work. He can't sit quietly because he is eager to do more. This is not intentional disruption. I can understand him; he is anxious not to fail. Maybe he's afraid in other subjects. The whole class has a stigma of failure in the theoretical subjects.

Math teacher: - (sneering), I believe they have a 'block' in almost every subject.

English teacher: - (reflectively), From what you have just said, I understand that the boy, and maybe the others too, are either frightened by the theoretical subjects or simply disinterested. If that is the case, why keep them here? They have good hands; let them go out and work.

Mechanics teacher: - I believe that we have to lower the standards so as not to fail them. The students should feel that they are capable, and then gradually we can demand more and more. We should start with a few things only, just to show them what they can do.

Team leader: - (in admiration), You talk so beautifully...

Mechanics teacher: - Every lesson, we could focus on one boy, take him in hand.

Math teacher: - (doubtful), And what do you do with the whole class?.

Mechanics teacher: - It's difficult, but with a bit of love and care, we can surely build up his knowledge and trigger his interest...

Biology teacher: - Yigal's problem is that he doesn't submit any written work.

Music teacher: - I teach them about notes and rhythm, real abstract concepts. When I see that Nitza has done well, I call out, "Nitza hand over your paper. Now that's very good; you get 10 for it". Then they all want to get 10.

Team leader: - Does Yigal submit a paper too?

Music teacher: - Certainly.

Team leader: - (perplexed), So why doesn't that happen in the other subjects?

Hydraulics teacher: - He started well in my subject, adapted really well, but in the past month he has stopped working. He got 30 in the exam. Since then, he has stopped. I have tried talking to him but with no effect.

Mechanics teacher: - He is a very sensitive boy. He reacts strongly even to a kind word. He cannot confront anger; when he is told off, he just closes up. I suggest we invite him here, show him how we work, how interested and keen we are for him to learn. We should give him just one problem, one exercise at a time, and challenge him to do it, promising a good mark if he succeeds.

This excerpt illustrates the unique dynamics that developed in the team between the vocational teachers and the general subject teachers. It reflects how the team interaction succeeded in tearing down the stereotyped image that had been pinned to the boy and in developing a deeper vision and understanding of a complex situation. The mechanics teacher, a key figure in this session, describes in simple words his theory-in-action, a theory that gains its validity through *practice,* by its usefulness in helping him act more intelligently and skillfully. (Elliott 1981) His professional superiority is realized by the academic teachers who disregard his lower status in terms of learning and are ready to listen and accept his advice. The first to admit that her eyes had been opened to a fuller picture of Yigal is the English teacher as she actually starts to reflect upon her action.

Responding to the team leader's request, the mechanics teacher starts isolating various factors in his teaching that could be of value to the others such as, adopting a personal approach to each of the students, understanding their fear of failure, etc.. This breaking down of 'tools' from the situation to make them usable with different materials (Bamberger and Schon 1983) generates new insight. It enhances the participants' divergent thinking, liberating them from their 'tunnel vision' (Miller 1982) towards a fuller conception of the multi-faceted situation. This is the first step in a personal growth process that continues in a spiral, and which should bring them closer to the solution of the basic problem, that is, how to enhance significant learning in low-ability classes.

The Third Year

In the third year, the school decided to carry on with the self-renewal project independently. The model of weekly team sessions in the low-ability classes, which had become established, would now be supervised by the school counselor. Meanwhile, an in-service course for teachers (INSET) was opened by the university, for teachers from different schools with the aim of disseminating the process of self-renewal. (More will be said about this INSET later.)

Two active team leaders from the self-renewal project who were also participants in the INSET course decided to invite their colleagues to visit their school towards the end of the year to learn about the project in a more direct way. The visit included meeting the project teams, primarily the teachers who taught in low-ability classrooms, observing these classrooms at work and, finally, interviewing students in order to obtain their feedback on the project. The following excerpt is taken from the recorded meeting with the teachers. It opens with a description of the final integrative assignment initiated in the low-ability classes.

Math teacher: - I see the final project on 'Beer Sheva, the town' as a great   success. We organized a full-day excursion of students and teachers to learn about our town. Our group decided to study the old Turkish bridge. In collaboration with the teacher for design and strength of materials, the basic principles of construction were learned and a model of the bridge was made for the exhibition. The history of the town was taught by the history teacher who also exhibited their learning with the aid of diagrams. Two life-sized models of soldiers were dressed by the girls as part of their fashion and sewing classes. Each of the teachers was able to develop real learning activities in his/her subject area. It was a joint effort with good results.

Hydraulics teacher: - We began with a class that was jointly integrated around the negative objective of anti-learning. Our only chance was to create a similar unit of teachers integrated around a clear policy of action. To tell the truth, at the beginning, each of us was ready to give up and save our efforts for a more deserving class – one that would appreciate our work. But once we collaborated, things started moving with promising results, which, in turn, motivated us to continue. Today, before their graduation, I can see we have opened up a new road of opportunities for them. There are good vocational courses in their subject and those who want to continue their studies will be able to do so after their military service. They have a good enough basis. We have done a good job here, which motivates me to go on working in this way in other classes.

Fashion design teacher: - We went through a long period of difficulties: antagonism, absenteeism. I didn't think it would work. I believe the turning point was when they felt our close and united surveillance ... They stopped dropping out of lessons and became more involved and interested. The whole atmosphere in the class changed. They became more open; they listened, and asked questions. When there was a problem, we talked about it.

Counselor: - I feel that the picture drawn here is a bit too rosy and I want to remind you of the difficult times – the days when despair took hold of us, when suddenly out of the blue, something happened and seemed to disrupt all that had been achieved.

Guest: - Could you give us an example?

Counselor: - After weeks of preparation, the whole class abstained from the school party. We saw this as a real setback. Our real test was to cope with the disappointment. Each one of us had some breakdown moments. As a team, we were quick to offer support in such moments and, by doing so, strengthen our colleagues as well as ourselves as a supportive group. The night we put up the exhibition, the place was all lit up and festive. I looked at the students and at ourselves and felt the joy of mutual creation. Everyone cared. If it hadn't been for our united effort, we wouldn't have succeeded. As for the weekly team sessions, we took them very seriously. It meant working, reading, and trying to improve the definition of our problems and our objectives. It was very serious work.

Guest: - Could you give us an example of the group's supportive assistance?

Mechanics teacher: - I remember a whole session dealing with a problem posed by the teacher of automation. He complained that no matter how much he explained, they just didn't understand!

After a long discussion we were able to show him that these 17 and 18 year-olds needed concrete examples. We also helped him prepare some learning materials to illustrate the abstract issues.

English teacher: - I also had my breakdown moment. It was then that I came to understand their need for immediate awards. Since then I have learned to break my material into small units with an assignment at the end of each which would grant them a mark.

Hebrew teacher: - It isn't a question of 'holding them in tight'. They actually need these concrete confirmations from us to assure them that their work is good.

The encounter speaks for itself. The teachers try to summarize, each from his or her point of view, their collaborative endeavor. Such summary discussions have a tendency to become euphoric, allowing the teachers to get carried away by their recollections. Yet I feel that the teachers expressed authentic optimism after having achieved something, they originally thought was impossible.

What started out as confrontation between two parties gradually changed to mutual understanding and real communication between teachers and students. Their achievement at having opened up an opportunity, a way for their students, implies also an opening of a new way of teaching. Discovering this new way of handling actually motivated them to continue. A final point of interest is the supportive function of the team – a point that was naturally stressed by the counselor.

Meeting the Students

The guest teachers were keen to collect feedback from the students themselves. A joint meeting was organized. Before assembling, small groups of guest teachers and students were formed to get aquainted. They then sat down together in the plenary to share information. The following excerpt is taken from the plenary meeting:

- She made me realize how much she and also the other teachers cared for us.

- If it hadn't been for her, I wouldn't have stuck to it. She managed to show me that it's all for my own benefit, and not for anybody else's.
- I felt good in this class. I became interested in the subject (mechanics) and anyway I didn't want to go where I would have had to sweat harder.
- In the final project, teachers and students worked together, backing one another up. The girls helped with the sewing and hanging. It was a good project.

The guest teachers were highly impressed by the students' friendly and open attitudes, their ability to express themselves and, above all, by their positive attitudes to the school, their class, and their teachers. The main theme, expressed in many variations, was that they liked the school and felt adjusted in the classroom.

It sounded like the best answer that could be expected to the problem which, two years previously, had launched the whole process: "How to change student antagonism toward school and thus hopefully improve their school performance".

Discussion

The self-renewal project, which was implemented in a large comprehensive school, began as an intervention that was invited by the school with the aim of handling a process which they themselves had initiated. We were called in to help and our goal was to change the teachers' perception of their role from that of instrumental teachers, passively accepting and implementing established school norms, towards that of developmental teachers, more actively involved in school policy-making.

Aware of implementation difficulties reported in the literature, we decided to run the first year as a trial activity, to observe, reflect, and prepare for change. As a result of this pilot run, a 'Heuristic-model for problem solving' was developed, involving teams of teachers in problem-solving processes. The teams served as optimal media for change in which the teachers developed their reflective and diagnostic abilities and learned to define their theories-of-action. Generating their own professional knowledge, they became more autonomous, reducing their dependency on the authority of knowledge. They developed a more tentative, less absolute perception of knowledge and reached a higher level of professional development (Glassberg and Oja 1981).

Through the project, we, the researchers gained a better understanding of the teachers' professional growth process. We learned that it is a slow process that requires patience on the part of the researcher, offering no instant or glamorous success. On the other hand, the outcomes supported our assumption that teachers in groups are capable of learning research skills and becoming involved in action-research.

Our final hypothesis was concerned with the school as an institution. We hypothesized that teachers' personal growth would be coupled with institutional growth. Yet when evaluating school change, we were faced with conflicting interpretations. Judging from the number of voluntary teams and participants, the project seemed to be declining. It seemed that although the model of activation functioned well, the teachers were not keen to use it. Naturally, we tended to have reservations about the capacity of the project to induce institutional change. A completely different interpretation was offered by the school. Both teachers and management regarded the project as a success, as an instrument of significant change. This was no halo-effect: Based upon evidence of change within the school, changes at the management level seemed to be the most impressive. The management perceived itself as being more sensitive and efficient, having improved both its 'receptiveness' and 'responsiveness', two criteria used as measures of self-renewal (Schmuck et al. 1974).

This brought us, the research team, to reflect on our action. In doing so, the first thing we realized was that the original pyramid-structured model of intervention, based on problem-solving teams supervised by an external consultant, gave a biased representation of the actual situation, especially with respect to information flow and control. We believe that a new conception is called for, in which the school is regarded as a system; a system consisting of various subsystems, one of which is the research team functioning as an integral part of the whole. Accordingly, knowledge, instead of flowing from top to bottom, is generated independently in each team and diffused through unknown and unexpected routes. The research team seen as part of the whole is no more the sole controller of the process.

Perceiving the school as a system leads to a deeper understanding of the flow variables: the different processes of personal and organi-zational change. Instead of operating in a sequential order (for example, personal change initiating institutional change, and so on), we suggested a systemic model containing feedback loops and coupled processes. Such a model offers a better explanation of the richness of existing and potential interactions.

In conclusion, the self-renewal project developed into action-research. It involved all those responsible for the practice – teachers, management and the research team – in the four strategies of action: implementation, observation, reflection and change.

The LAHAV (Self-Renewal in the School) Project

Having gained experience and confidence in action-reasearch, not merely as a methodology but also as a new educational orientation applicable to teachers' professional development and to systemic educational change, we were ready to widen our horizon. Our new extended project was called LAHAV (standing in Hebrew for "Self-Renewal in the School"). It involved five different schools and was sponsored by the Ministry of Education.

The framework of the project consisted of two-tiered in-service courses: (1) a central university INSET (in-service course for teachers), which I facilitated, consisting of five teams of key teachers each from the five participating schools, and (2) school-based INSETs, which were gradually established by these key teachers in their respective schools and which were also facilitated by them.

This new framework represents a more systemic macro-conception of educational change and development. It is based on a dialogic metaphor between the university and the field, in other words, collaboration between school teachers and university researchers. Consistent with the first project of school self-renewal, we were interested in the interplay between the process of institutional development and that of a personal-professional development of the participants as two coupled processes.

The participating schools were of different types: the original comprehensive school (with its three years of experience in the project) which served as a pilot school; a religious comprehensive school; a vocational high school for management, and an elementary school (all in the same town), as well as another comprehensive school situated in Yeruham, a small development town in the Negev desert.

The research team was enlarged to include five graduate students, each responsible for a particular school. Their role was to accompany the school-based INSET activities and collect data, consisting mainly of the transcripts of the various group meetings.

Institutional Development

The participating teachers in the central university INSET were all key figures chosen by their school management. They were to act as delegates of the new rationale in their respective schools. Thus, the central INSET served also as a medium for inter-school communication, triggering an ongoing interchange of ideas and experiences among the different schools.

As team leaders, they facilitated the school-based INSETs (SB-INSET), each of which functioned as an independent autonomous learning group. (Herbst 1976) Each team chose an area or issue (usually one conceived by them as a source of discontent), diagnosed an essential (often hidden) problem, generated working hypotheses and suggested ways of change. After experimenting or testing these hypotheses, in most cases, they were adopted by the school as institutional improvements or change.

The SB-INSET can also be seen as a framework for engaging groups of teachers in institutional learning processes (Argyris and Schon 1978), a framework for involving them in democratic deliberations in which their school's educational assumptions are questioned, where mismatches between ideologies and between the structure or function of the school are brought up and discussed openly in order to be resolved. In this respect, the participating teachers were actually taking an active part in school decision-making processes and reformulation of its policies within those areas that they chose to deal with. Institutional learning and development can be thus regarded as a process of 'school-democratization' in which the bureaucratic hierarchical model of organization gradually changes into a system or network model (Herbst 1976). More will be said on this later.

Personal Professional Development

On the personal level, all participant teachers underwent a process of professional growth within their groups. They learned to reflect 'on' and 'in' action and gradually develop as reflective teachers. (Schon 1983) As such, their instrumental orientation, in the sense of following a particular technique or routine, gradually became more open to trial, experimentation and constant modification. We assumed that in the future, such teachers would recruit their reflective thinking and self-direction rather than function in an automatic manner.

As reflective teachers, they also became more self-aware, more attuned to their inner self, beliefs, or ideologies, which could no longer remain as labels or cliches but needed to be examined and re-examined in practice. This is what I mean by the term 'authentic teacher'– authenticity in the sense of fuller congruence between the teacher's beliefs and basic assumptions, on the one hand, and his or her professional behavior, on the other.

Authentic teachers are more free to use their personalities as their main vehicle for teaching (Morris 1965). Acting as *persons* (as opposed to functioning as role players), they are able to regard their students as individuals who have their own rights. As such, they are able to maintain a more democratic personal relationship with them. In their respectful stance towards their students as persons, morality is also achieved.

A respectful stance, as a basis for a personal relationship between teacher and student, does not necessarily imply a lassez-faire approach.   An ostensive non-directive role may not be helpful for students and, in some cases, it may even be harmful. The teacher's task is to create an optimal relationship for joint learning: collaboration which acknowledges the teacher as an experienced adult and, in this sense, not equal to the student and, at the same time, a relationship that acknowledges the students as young persons with the full right to express themselves.

To illustrate what we mean by the two interconnected processes – institutional and personal-professional development, let us focus on the 'Unsetting in Math' project in the Re-ut Elementary School.

The 'Unsetting in Math' Project

First, a few background words: 'Setting' means dividing a class into (usually three) homogenous groups based on level of achievement in a particular subject. In Israel, setting is used in three main subjects, Hebrew, Math and English as a foreign language. This measure was introduced in the early 60s in order to provide an answer to the growing heterogeneity of the school population following mass immigration. The dominant 'melting-pot' policy at the time was to integrate the different socio-cultural groups as quickly as possible.   It was assumed that 'setting' would help meet the students' particular needs more effectively and with the aid of new teaching methods, gaps would soon diminish.

In the Re-ut school, as in all elementary schools in the town, setting was carried out in the top two (7th and 8th) grades. However, the Re-ut school staff were particularly sensitive to the negative effect of setting on low-ability students. They felt that instead of advancing, setting 'fixated' them. This formed the background to their initiative to experiment 'unsetting' in Math.

As part of the LAHAV project, a team of four math teachers was formed with the school counselor acting as team leader. It was decided to start experimenting un-setting in the three classes of the 7th grade; in other words, to teach math in the regular heterogeneous context of their respective classrooms. In addition, a small budget from the school's inspector enabled the establishment of three 'supportive-groups' of 13 students each. The idea was to let the students decide whether they needed two extra weekly periods of math teaching and, accordingly, choose to participate in the supportive group. Much to everyone's surprise, the groups formed on this voluntary basis, did not consist only of weak students, but included also high- and medium-level achievers. In other words, the supportive groups were quite heterogeneous (like the regular classes), consisting mixed-ability students.

The team began its group work by questioning the effectiveness of setting in math. Intuitively, the team members felt that fixation stemmed not from labeling the students as high, medium or low achievers, but by creating three different curricula which, in turn, minimized the mobility of the students from lower to higher sets.

As a group of experienced math teachers, the participants soon realized that organizational reframing from homogenous to hetero-geneous contexts was not sufficient. As put by one math teacher:

- Organizationally, the plan looked fine and simple...but when confronted with 36 mixed-ability students, I realized we had no idea how to teach them...

Judy, the counselor, who was also the leading spirit of the project, was not a math teacher. She was to teach in the supportive groups. The project became her field of research in the framework of her graduate studies. In her MA thesis, submitted two years later, she reflects on the choice of math for experimenting mixed-ability-teaching (MAT):

- Because schools and society consider math as being the number one subject, whoever gets high marks in math is labeled clever, or capable. Hence, students who achieve high grades in the mixed ability classes are considered clever in the eyes of their teachers, parents, as well as in their own eyes. You see, I had that need to **demystify math...** (Zamir 1990)

In the LAHAV project, unlike our previous pilot project (described above), we had no direct access to the teachers' group work, which they insisted they would run independently. True to our policy to let the team dictate their own terms, we could not audio-tape their weekly group meetings and, therefore, we had to look for other sources of data in order to trace their learning process, such as interviews, classroom observations and, eventually, Judy's MA thesis. All these enabled our follow-up of the teachers' process of learning and curriculum development.

The Math Teachers' Teamwork

One of the first issues discussed in the group was the question of who would be the target population. After careful consideration, their decision fell on set B. Judy provides the rationale for this decision:

- In previous years, we formed the sets by classifying the kids according to their achievements their test scores at the end of grade 6 (11 years old). We creamed off the good ones to set A and, in a similar manner, the weak ones were assigned to set C. There was no criterion for set B except for not being in set A or

C. I was sure that among them there were many whose learning potential was no different from that of set A kids. My hypothesis was that by unsetting, by removing the label, these kids would be able to reach higher levels of achievement.... (ibid)

Facing her new role as teacher of math in the supportive-groups, Judy asked her colleagues for guidance: Could they show her how to approach the first topic in the syllabus? What followed this innocent request, we learnt through an interview with Tirza, the head math teacher:

- Judy, the counselor asked us for our strategy, the way we approach this particular topic in the 7th grade, so we all started throwing out our ideas of how to teach this specific topic. ... a kind of 'brainstorming' ... Much to our surprise, we discovered that we four teachers had four different ways - different approaches to the same topic. Moreover, after more discussion, we realized that we each understood this teaching task in a different way ... By reflecting upon this newly discovered phenomenon, we were able to elaborate on the subject of 'different representations of knowledge' which, in turn, generated new questions, such as, "Could we assume that each person had his or her own unique representation of knowledge, or could each representation be classified according to given criteria?" "Does this apply to the kids, too? If so, they would also have different ways of constructing knowledge".

This revelation led the teachers to use their meetings for developing different work sheets based on their alternative approaches, and to implement them in their classrooms. A whole range of work sheets was presented in the classroom, allowing individual students to choose what appealed or made more sense to them. Reflecting upon this stage, the team realized what their hidden curriculum was:

- You see, at this stage we were implicitly suggesting through our teaching that there are different ways of solving problems ... Even in math, there is no one-and-only-one correct answer... (Zamir 1990)

Thus, they continued collaboratively to produce some six to eight work sheets for every new topic which, when shared between them, meant less of a burden (of preparation) for each.

By the second year, the teachers were in a position to make revisions in the curriculum for the new cohort of 7th graders joining the project.   At the same time, they continued experimenting with the 8th graders.I found that at this stage they were much more articulate about the process, understanding their own as well as their colleagues' different mathematical logic.

Their newly gained insight is clearly illustrated in the following excerpt, also taken from Judy's dissertation. It dwells on a group interaction in which the teachers strove to understand each others' logic through each participant's personal associations and, finally, to discuss the implications of all this for their teaching:

- The mathematical concept of 'numerical-form' was defined as a combination of variables, numbers and mathematical operations, all of which represent a number. We started throwing examples of numerical-forms such as $2x + 4$; $4(x - 3y)$.
Teacher A associated numerical-form with a cake-form to which one can add whatever one feels like (give different values to the variables) so that in one case, it would be a chocolate cake, and in another, a fruit cake.
Teacher B claimed that in her mind, a numerical-form was associated with a recipe, not a cake-form. In a recipe, the proportions between the different ingredients are always maintained, so that the difference between the cakes is merely in their size.
Teacher C did not use the cake metaphor. For her, a numerical-form was associated with geometry; for example, $4a$ is a numerical-form representing the circumference of a square; $2a + 2b$ stands for a circumference of an oblong, a paralleloid, or, in the case of $a = b$, it represents the circumference of a square too. (Zamir 1990)

Judy concludes by adding her personal insight to the story:

- By trying to understand each other's logic, we came nearer to understanding the possible alternative logic of the students and what difficulties of understanding might arise from each of the above representations... In the class, we were now less intent on producing more alternatives: Instead, we saw our task as opening the students up and encouraging them to come forth with their own associations...(ibid)

Teaching in the Supportive Groups

Judy's idea of a supportive group was to have an informal facilitating medium of learning, to strengthen the students' confidence and enhance their self-esteem. Precautions were taken against the possibility of these supportive groups being negatively labeled as a framework for '*helping the weak and poor*'. This was the main reason for granting the students the choice of whether to participate or not. The decision not to participate, of students who could have done with extra teaching, was respected.

In order to gain some direct information on classroom interaction and learning processes, we suggested that an observer be introduced into the classroom as an 'extra pair of eyes' for the teacher. This idea did not appeal to the teachers; they were suspicious of it. Judy was the first to allow such an observer visit her (supportive) groups. The following excerpt, taken from the observer's notes, illustrates the groups' unique learning climate:

- Teaching was held in a most informal way. Thirteen students were seated in a half-circle and they were encouraged to work in teams and consult each other during the lesson. No homework was issued; no testing or grading methods were used. The atmosphere created was an antithesis to that usually associated with school and, in particular, math teaching. Instead of driving for one single correct solution to a problem posed, the teacher asked the students to come forth with different solutions...

Because the supportive groups were also heterogeneous with regard to level of achievement, the 'multiple-representations-of-knowledge' way of teaching was applied there too: The teacher presented each new topic in various ways, creating a better chance for each student to understand; providing a key that would fit each learner's style of learning.

This idea is vividly illustrated by the observer who happened to overhear the following conversation between two students:

- You have to find the appropriate screw to fit this hole and, maybe, as is usually the case, you can find more than one that fits...

To this Judy adds in her dissertation:

- The teacher's task is thus seen in a completely different way. He or she has to find 150 different approaches to the same content, in order to cope with the students' different perceptions. (see Wilson, Shulman and Richert 1987)

The next step, which sprang naturally from this basic framework, had to do with *timing*. Each new topic in the curriculum was introduced in the supportive group *prior* to its introduction in the regular class. This measure allowed the students of the supportive group to become better acquainted with new topics, building up their self-confidence.

This change in the student's learning behavior is observed by one of the math teachers in the following excerpt:

- I was completely surprised by T. today. Usually, you know her; she sits passively, waiting for the others to supply her with the answer. Much to my astonishment, she voluntarily worked the whole procedure of the solution on the blackboard... You should have seen the surprise and sense of contentment in the class...Walking back proudly to her seat, she was radiant.

Judy sums up her view of the change, or rather the professional development of the group of math teachers:

- As a result of our changed conception of our role as teachers, on the one hand, and our simultaneous classroom interaction, on the other, another idea of heterogeneity, almost a parallel process of change grew. We realized that like us, the students too had qualitatively different ways of understanding; that is, that the differences in their knowledge were not merely quantitative, in terms of content, (which is the underlying logic behind setting into high medium and low sets). By overcoming the idea of a hierarchy of understanding, or hierarchy of learning, our approach to the students became much more egalitarian, and I believe more tolerant. This basic change of approach was somehow relayed through our teaching to the classroom, making the students more open and forthcoming with their difficulties. It was as though we were finally able to admit that each person, teacher or student has his or her legitimate logic of understanding. I believe this change created a stronger impact upon their learning than our original supportive approach, advocated in terms of humanistic, interpersonal values only...

(Zamir and Keiny 1980)

Learning from Classroom Observations –
A Reflective Dialogue

Only in the second year of the project were the participating teachers able to open up and discuss their difficulties less defensively. Nevertheless, they still clung to the image of the classroom as their private territory, closed to trespassers.

Judy, the first to allow Avi the observer to (what she termed) 'participate' in her supportive groups, soon learned to actually benefit from his observational information. Moreover, a kind of a partnership developed between them whereby she actually directed his observations to issues that were of interest to her. Slowly, thanks also to Avi's patient and tactful behavior, he managed to gain the other teachers' confidence and observe their classrooms, too.

The three-pronged method that he developed was to consult the teacher before the actual observation, to observe and, finally, use the observational data as a basis for a reflective dialogue with the teacher. The dialogues were recorded, transcribed, and fed back to the teachers for further deliberation.

The following example, taken from one of the early observations of Judy's supportive group, illustrates Avi's method of observation:

Avi opens by asking Judy to describe her way of teaching in this particular group. In response, she automatically recites the three main principles of her rationale:

1) Every new topic is to be dealt with in the group before being introduced to the whole class.
2) Boundaries are defined for each topic in order to minimize ambi-guity.
3) Math is 'demystified'.

Avi focuses his observations on these three points, collecting evidence to substantiate them. He then shares his data with Judy. For example, he cites phrases from her 'teacher talk':

- I am sure you can handle it yourself...
- Look how simple it really is..
- I told you you'd understand it, remember?

These, he suggests, substantiate her idea of demystification of math, especially as compared to the way math is commonly introduced, as the most difficult subject in school.

His observational data serve also to illuminate more tacit aspects of her teaching. For example:

- Each of the students was working on his/her learning task. Y. got up and walked over to show the teacher his work. S. and T. consulted each other. I noticed that they were dealing with different learning tasks. A little later, two boys were at the blackboard, each working on a different exercise, at his end of the blackboard...

Judy was surprised to discover that she had actually been indulging in 'differential learning tasks'. Reflecting upon this, she says it must have become 'second nature' in her teaching style.

They then move on to reflect on the learning climate of the supportive groups. Avi's observational data indicate free and informal student behavior, such as walking about, talking among themselves, etc. At the same time, a serious attitude to the work at hand, shared by teacher and students alike, was observed. The social interactions among the students did not reflect just playing around.

It is now Judy's turn to relate her observational experience in the math teachers' team. She admits that through Avi's *extra pair of eyes,* she was made aware about many sides of her teaching that she was not conscious of, not all of them favorable. For example, she was made aware that she did not divide her attention equally among the students. She also became aware that she was less tolerant with some students, whom she admitted she had labeled as 'not worth her while'. Impressed by these findings, Miri, one of the other math teachers, invites Avi to observe her classroom and follow the observation with a reflective dialogue.

Thus, as the teachers gradually gained more confidence in the process, they learned to use the 'observer service' and planned the observation sessions to fit in with their own preferred schedule. At one point, they directed Avi to focus on three particular students in order to try and disclose their learning methods and help them arrive at a better understanding of the logic underlying their thinking. Avi 'shadowed' the three, observed their learning behavior in the supportive group as well as in the regular classroom, attempting to trace the effect of the former on their changed learning behavior in the regular class.

This led to the construction of a 'typology' of the supportive group learners based on the five criteria: involvement, autonomy, self-confidence, initiative, and communication or interaction (for more details, see Faital anf Keiny 1990).

In the third year of the project, we were requested by the principal and her small management group to evaluate the project. Our strategy for evaluation was to act as both external and internal evaluators. We collected data, presented our evaluation report, which was based upon both qualitative and quantitative data, analyzed it, and wrote a report to be presented to the whole school.

The report indicated quite clearly that this small group of teachers had actually achieved their declared goals. By developing a new method of math teaching, they had produced a new mixed-ability-teaching (MAT) curriculum (instead of the three different curricula that were taught in the sets) and, thereby, eliminated, actually *counteracted the fixation effect that was caused by setting.*

Based on the students' mathematical achievement in their final exams, we were able to show that 40 percent of the students who would have been classified as set B, had managed to graduate from elementary school with an A score in math.   As a consequence, they were admitted to academically oriented classes (where many of them continued to make good progress). This meant a very radical change that opened a new range of opportunities for their future.

Two More Examples of School-Based INSET

The case of the Re-ut primary school presented above is but one example of the work of the LAHAV project.   Each of the participating schools developed its own story, its unique interpretation of the rationale and its particular fields of action. My second example, based on the experience of the vocational high school for management, is a far less successful story.

The principal of the school was very enthusiastic at the beginning, welcoming our idea of self-renewal and collaboration. A group of five key teachers were sent to participate in the central INSET.   In the second year, they each became a team leader, facilitating an SB-INSET group of teachers. Each group chose its own topic, for example, 'Changing the [highly demanding] school testing system', which consumed most of the classroom teaching time and, as a result, instead of learning, students were constantly preparing for the next exam.   Another team worked on 'Improving the teacher-student relationship', with the aim of creating a less formal school climate.

By the end of the second year, we were able to conceptualize their progress within their different teams and write a very positive report. At a special meeting of the school management and the project's team leaders, we gave a presentation based on the written report. Much to our surprise, the principal's abrupt response was: "I had not realized that LAHAV was a 'school democratization' project and I have no intention of following this direction..."

That was the end of the story of our partnership with this school.

My third example is taken from the religious comprehensive school. Under the umbrella of the principal's defined goal, 'Improving the school image', the entire school staff was involved in the implementation of the project. Four objectives were specified by the principal:

(a) to deepen religious education,
(b) to redefine the school norms in religious terms,
(c) to improve teaching strategies,
(d) to cultivate the aesthetic physical image of the school.

The four SB-INSET groups formed, served as medium for achieving these objectives. It should be emphasized that all of these steps were prescribed by the principal. The group responsible for improving the aesthetic image of the school began its activity in the summer vacation by redecorating, sewing curtains, hanging up pictures and plants, etc. Their implicit assumption was that their message to the students would be best conveyed by creating a new aesthetic reality in time for the begining of the school year. It soon became evident that the teachers' strong drive to change had been at the expense of group reflection and deeper understanding of the process. In a more subtle sense, it counteracted the notion of the teachers taking responsibility for the renewal of their school policy.

This issue of responsibility was symptomatic in the other teams, too. It was highlighted in our first year report with respect to the relationship between teachers and students. We pointed out that the center of responsibility was very much with the teachers in that they prescribed norms of behavior (regarding religious or aesthetic aspects of their agenda).   Instead of involving the students in decisions, they were merely disciplined to clean the place or behave appropriately without developing a sense of the school as *their* place for them to cultivate.

Unlike the above example, the impact of our report was to trigger the principal and participating teachers toward reflecting on their actions and to formulate more clearly what they meant by improving the school image. We assumed that by triggering reflection and deliberation, they would be better able to decide on future courses of action.

To conclude, the above examples illustrate three different interpretations of the project by three different schools. Collaboration, which was understood as an asset in the Re-ut school, was conceived by the vocational school principal as a threat to his status. In the religious school, with its implicit autocratic ideology, the young energetic principal tried to impose collaboration or, to use Hargreave's term, to create 'contrived collaboration' (Hargreaves 1994). Improving the school image by decorating and making curtains reveals the principal's metaphor of 'the school as our home' and the teachers as good parents. However, the teachers, habituated to comply with authority, never stopped to question their norms their metaphors, or their action. The same model was relayed in their classrooms, substantiating our assumption that responsibility cannot be taught. Teachers need to exercise responsibility themselves in order to be able to grant responsibility to their students.

A last note before closing this chapter has to do with our own learning: The richness of the stories revealed in the different school-based INSETS furnished us with a deeper understanding of our systemic conception. We came to see the system of education as consisting of various subsystems that interact with each other in unexpected multidimensional ways, both overt and covert. We also learned that action-reasearch cannot be imposed on teachers or schools; they have to be willing to question their routine, experiment new ways, and create the necessary collaborative frameworks. Accordingly, the concept of school resistance does not imply physical or feasible resistance. We see it rather as a *conceptual barrier*. To impliment school change or self-renewal, a *conceptual change* from linear to circular systemic thinking is required.

Chapter 3

Teachers' Professional Development as a Process of Dialectical Reflection in the Group

Having gained a more systemic understanding of school change and development, we felt the need to move from the macro-back to the micro-level. The experience of various forms of teachers' group work, each focusing on a particular problem, each weaving a unique and different story, led to the question whether a common scheme could be identified, a model of teachers' group learning. We felt the need to follow up and examine the actual process of learning in the group more closely; to turn the lens away from school self-renewal and the process of school development and focus on the coupled process of the personal professional development of teachers.

This could be achieved either by approaching the accumulated case studies' data from a new perspective, or by adopting a new method of analysis. I preferred to go back to the field with a new pair of spectacles and initiate a new group process. As I saw it, the two alternatives reflected two different conceptions of my role – researcher versus facilitator. Re-examining the old data from a new perspective would entail only a change in my role as a researcher, whereas a new intervention process that opened up new opportunities of interaction with the group would entail a change in my role as facilitator as well. The latter was also more in line with my conception of action-research in that it allowed for the application of our already accumulated knowledge in our practice of teaching.

The case study presented in this chapter is about my work as a facilitator of a group of 10 teachers who formed the teaching staff of a vocational, low-achieving, 10th grade class.

The Group

The participants of the group consisted of the entire teaching staff of one particular 10th grade vocational class (of 22 boys and girls): the teachers of Hebrew, Scripture, English, Math, History, Geography, Mechanics, Sewing and Fashion Design, as well as the head teacher of the 10th grade cohort and myself, as facilitator. A regular weekly double period (90 minutes) was allotted for group meetings, which I saw as indication that the management was serious about in backing our group work. The proceedings of the meetings, which were audio taped and transcribed, and then handed out to all the participants for further reflection, also formed the database for our analysis of the group process.

The explicit aim of the group was 'to develop more meaningful learning in the classroom'. In my opening remarks to the members of the group , I explained my notion of a joint task group, arguing that meaningful learning could not be achieved by each party separately but required the collaboration of all of us – practitioners and researchers.

The Process

It was agreed that we would start by acquiring more information about each student. Thus, the first three meetings were devoted to a preliminary survey of the students. Personal information was supplied by the home-teacher, who also had access to the students' personal files. After completing this round of 'reconnaissance', each participant (in the fourth meeting) was asked to formulate a 'working question' that he or she was keen to pursue. Following are a few examples of the participants' questions:

- How is it possible to develop the students' moral sensitivity as well as their thinking capacity?
- How should we handle disciplinary cases that entailed the breaking of norms?
- How can we cultivate a love for books amongst these pupuils?
- How can we turn them from passive into active learners?

These working questions could be divided roughly into two categories, one dealing with learning issues and the other with classroom behavior. Indeed, they could be seen as 'symptoms' of two cardinal problems, the first, "How to develop more meaningful learning in the classroom?" and the second, "How to deal with norms and educational values?".

My original plan was to promote an unstructured, open-ended process. However, the group, without taking any formal decision, plunged forward into a pattern, which, once repeated, became an interesting cyclic learning process.

A teacher would volunteer to voice his or her working question, which usually stemmed from a deep feeling of discontent, asking the group to partake in a process of inquiry. Classroom observations and other methods of data collection would follow and the various findings would be triangulated. Thus, reflection in the group would be triggered from different angles or different reference points and new understanding would emerge with respect to the specific question under discussion.
To illustrate this type of collaborative learning process, I have chosen four such 'learning cycles' (presented in their chronological order).

First Learning Cycle

The first to volunteer was Ricky, the home-teacher of this particular class, who taught fashion-design. She began by relating the following episode, which actually formed the background to her question:

...The relationship between me and the girls is open and friendly ....Imagine how shocked I was when they told me that they felt

totally unprepared for the exam. How could there be such a gap
between my notion of having covered the curriculum and their
claim that they were not prepared.... Is it possible that there are
some 'blind spots' in my teaching which I am unaware of ? ...What
is the cause of this discrepancy? That is why I decided to take the
'first leap' .... Maybe observation of my class work will reveal the
faults in my teaching ...

Ricky's formulated working question had been, "How can we
ensure that the content that I teach is actually grasped by the
students?" She invited the group to observe her next lesson,
which was to deal with the topic of 'Fashion in the ancient
world: A comparison between Egypt and Greece'. Her teaching
performance revealed a high degree of confidence, absolute
control of classroom interactions, which was achieved in a most
pleasant and easy-going manner. Her 'ping-pong' style of
questioning restricted the girls' participation to answering her
questions. At the end of the lesson, she handed them a typed
sheet summing up the topic.

The group discussion that followed the observation opened
with hearty praise for Ricky's performance. They complimented
her for the friendly classroom climate, her clever use of different
visual aids, which helped illustrate and concretize abstract
concepts, etc. Gradually the feedback moved to a deeper level of
analysis:

- I learned quite a few new things today but as a student I doubt
  whether I would have been able to sum them up.
Ricky: - That is why I prepared the summing-up sheet myself...
  - ... I expect that as a student, I would copy your sheet mechanically,
  without really digesting the material.
- I thought that the topic was presented very well; the illustrations
  were vivid...
- I agree, but you know, I come from Russia, and that is how we
  taught there. Here, in the free world, in a democratic country,
  don't you think we should teach them to think and to develop their
  own ideas instead of just having to repeat what the teacher says...?

The deliberation continued in the next meeting. The group
examined samples of the girls' files with the aim of tracing their

understanding or lack of understanding of the teaching content. The idea was to try and follow up Ricky's teaching from the students' standpoint.   However, going through a sample of assignments, the teachers' attention was soon drawn to another aspect, to Ricky's method of assessment.

> - I find the structure of the test very different from that of the lesson. The questions are phrased in a completely different way.
> - I am more concerned about your system of marking. No written comments in the margin; only a numerical score (percent) at the end, which does not give a clue to the learner as to where he or she went wrong.
> - I find your questions very complex. Maybe you could split each into a series of more simple ones.

The discussion that followed focused on the issue of evaluation, in general, and on the teaching/learning role of assessments, in particular: How to help the learner become more aware of his or her mistakes, understand them and thus revise his or her knowledge; how assessing by carefully written margin notes can become a dialogue between teacher and learner and not merely a tool of judgment.

Three different aspects of Ricky's teaching were illuminated by the group:

> - Conceptually, the subject was presented as a one-and-only-truth.
> - On the pedagogical level, a teacher-centered and teacher-controlled orientation was used.
> - On the assessment level, the teacher's motives and objectives were not made clear to the students, which impeded their ability to learn from their own mistakes.

Although Ricky's problem was not yet solved, some valuable points had been highlighted by the observations and the dialectical process of reflection in the group. These were substantiated by relevant articles, which I had selected from the research literature.   Participants each chose an article and the following three group sessions were devoted to a more theoretical type of learning, each participant reporting his or her reading to the group.

This was just the beginning – the first learning cycle. The fact that it triggered more teachers to take on the challenge and voice their problems was for me the clearest sign of its success.

The Second Learning Cycle

Janet, the Scripture teacher was the second to volunteer. She too wanted to use the group observation in order to assess her teaching: "To what extent was it congruent with her goals and objectives? She chose to spell her pre-active planned objectives on the blackboard before the classroom observation, asking the group to use these when observing her classroom. We decided that each of us would focus on one particular objective.

The topic of the lesson was the story of Joseph in Egypt. Classroom observation was immediately followed by a group discussion. Excerpts from this discussion are presented in the following:

- I chose to focus on the level of the students' interest and I got a real surprise. You are in love with your teaching and you seem to infect them with this feeling. (voices of consent in the group).
- I focused on the issue of 'frames', the relation between the individual and the different frames and the need to adapt to them. I thought you handled it beautifully.
- I liked your method of inference, moving naturally from the story of Joseph to the authentic realities of today.
- I enjoyed your lesson ..., the way you listened to the students out of respect... and the way they reacted to it. I was amazed at A's ability to express himself. I never would have believed that he could be so eloquent and open...

The following meeting opened with the facilitator asking whether there was anything else Janet wanted us to comment on.

Janet: - You have said nothing about values, I would like to have your feedback on this issue: "To what degree were the values underlying the story actually absorbed by the students?"

Hebrew literature teacher: - This was precisely the objective I chose to focus on and that is why I chose to read, in my next meeting with the class, a story which describes (rather implicitly) a child's mental change; how he developed from a weakling into a courageous man. They immediately reacted to the word 'change' relating it to Joseph. This opened up a discussion on human beings being responsible for change versus the surrounding environment as the responsible factor, as in the case of Joseph. It seems to me that our joint effort made an impact. They moved easily from the scriptures to history, relating to the Dreyfus case as an external event that influenced Herzel, and back to our story of internal change.

History teacher: - I tried to trace the thinking events that occurred in your lesson. You started by reading the chapter, providing the general frame-work of the plot. Then you wrote down the facts of the story, in con-junction with the causes, or Joseph's traits. You then dealt with the students' stereotypic conceptions. Finally, I sensed the underlying dilemma that was there all along: How, as a religious teacher, you try to introduce critical and pluralistic thinking to your teaching of the Bible.

Janet: - Your comments are most important. Yet, I wonder how one can be aware and deal with each issue without disturbing the natural sequence of the lesson...

This second cycle indicates a higher level of reflection. It relates to different aspects of learning, such as how to deal with concept leaning, how to activate students' learning and, finally, how to trace students' thinking.

The participants are sensitive to Janet's attempts to connect ideas and concepts from the biblical text to relevant, real life situations of the students, to their personal conceptual field. On the affective level, they are quick to note her deep involvement in her subject matter and her ability to convey this in the classroom. The teachers commend her for the way she listens to the students, showing respect for their ideas.

An interesting, new aspect is introduced into the discussion by Dov, the history teacher. Having practiced Frankenstein's (1970) teaching methods for culturally deprived students, he is able to elicit deeper cognitive thinking in the group. This brings forth peer-learning as another dimension of the group work: the group as a learning medium in which individuals act simultaneously as teachers and as learners.

The Third Learning Cycle

The relation between the concrete and abstract aspects of learning, was the next issue which stemmed from Benny's focal question: "How can we integrate the students' concrete thinking, an area they seem to thrive in, with some abstract thinking?" The context was a sewing workshop, conducted by Benny, who taught the girls how to sew a skirt.

As observers, the group was fascinated by the classroom climate. The students were industrious, highly motivated, and seemed to derive real pleasure from the learning situation.

The following excerpt is taken from the discussion that followed the observation:

- efficient, well organized, relaxed atmosphere, but doesn't this kind of teaching lead to dependency rather than understanding?
Benny: - I follow a model, a specific framework that I have to stick to because it forms the necessary basis. Whoever wants to study further, can do so on this basis.
- They rigidly follow your instructions. I would have preferred them to understand the rules, to go beyond the concrete.
- I liked the way you transmitted your love of the profession. They res-ponded to this in a creative way.
- Say that tomorrow some kind of crazy fashion comes onto the scene. Would they be able to function, to operate?
- But surely, once they can apply their learning to different sizes (as was demonstrated in the workshop), it signifies their ability to think and not just to follow instructions.
Benny: - I try to encourage each of them to proceed according to his or her level. Some of them are not able to use more complex

thinking. I would not like to cause them to be discouraged or to lead them to despair.

- I have difficulty with the notion of a standard level for these students. I believe their overt ability may be lower than their potential, or covert ability. Isn't it our task to develop this potential and lead them to a higher level of abstract thinking...?

In this excerpt, I thought I could trace some of the theoretical reading undertaken by the group in the previous stage. I wondered whether the theoretical knowledge was slow to be integrated, or whether it *made sense* only when connected to the actual practice. This issue will be discussed later.

The Fourth Learning Cycle

The last and most significant 'learning-cycle' took place in the mechanics workshop. The group was invited by Yossi, the mechanics teacher, to observe his twelve male students, each working on a huge rotor, creating an object that they themselves had designed in advance.

The following excerpt is taken from the group discussion, which followed immediately after this observed activity.

Math teacher: - I feel that this visit was long overdue...As teachers of these students, we should have come here much earlier to see them in their own territory... It gave me a completely different view of their abilities.

English teacher: - I agree. They are like different people here. Their usual classroom behavior cannot be compared with this mature and responsible performance ...

Yossi: - Let's not make such a big deal of it! ... As for responsibility, I agree, ... we do place a lot of emphasis on this aspect. The equipment they handle here is very expensive...

Ricky: - Could you give us an outline of your schedule? How do you organize the day's activities? ...

Yossi: - Well, it is basically individual learning. First, each student has to complete his design in class and divide his plan of action into written stages. I then go over the stages with him before he is permitted to cut his piece of raw metal and start working on it.

Math teacher: - I admit, I am absolutely overwhelmed by your achievement... seeing them so highly motivated, independent and, above all, really enjoying their work. This goes so far beyond my achievements with the same students... I believe the secret lies in the relevancy of your subject, as compared to mine (and she adds reflexively) How about working together on a joint curriculum... one that would be anchored in a concrete assignment and serve as a basis for learning abstract mathematical concepts?

Benny: - I can see another advantage that has to do with the products' worth. ...The same, by the way, applies to the sewing class...

Yossi: - We make quite an issue of the product's worth. We calculate the costs. (turning to the math teacher) This could be something of interest for you, another common denominator for a joint curriculum.

Facilitator: - Oh, but they were doing much more than simple calculations. They were actually engaged in high order thinking operations.

Yossi: - What do you mean?

Facilitator: - I was watching U. handling the huge rotor while he explained how he worked the machine. For example, he said, "If you want to reduce by 1 mm, you compute 0.5 mm on the rotor". I realized he was actually translating the two-dimensional design or drawing into the three-dimensional object that he was operating on. I admit that I thought him incapable of such high level operational thinking, yet, here he was doing it so naturally...

History teacher: - I see so many advantages in this particular learning process: The objectives are very clear; the body is in rhythm with the mind; there is creativity... The question is whether we, the teachers of the more theoretical subjects, can adapt some of these components into our teaching?

Yossi: - Another advantage is the longer periods of time they spend here with us (as compared to the standard 45 minutes of a regular lesson). This gives us a better opportunity to get to know them... to build a closer relationship between teacher and student...

Benny: - I could say the same about my sewing workshop but I think you tend to forget the other side of the coin, the low prestige attached to our practical subjects. They resent being here. They are ashamed of belonging to the vocational stream.

Janet: - Yet you have managed to change this feeling ...you have actually succeeded in building positive attitudes instead.

English teacher: - We, the teachers of the so-called prestigious subjects, lose them. We fail them and they turn against us, gradually hating the subject, the school, and altogether resenting the idea of learning.

Math teacher: - For me personally, this was an eye-opening experience... as it was for all of us no doubt.... We have to take serious measures if we want to improve our teaching and its effect on the students. I keep thinking about developing an integrative curriculum unit, one that integrates mechanics with math, and perhaps with physics, too. I suggest we start working on it together and implement it on an experimental basis in this class next year.

Geography teacher: - I had a similar idea concerning my subject, geography. (turning to Benny the sewing teacher) What do you say? Could we also try to develop together a small curriculum unit, which would focus on the issue of 'scale', a most fundamental concept in both of our subjects?

This excerpt serves to illuminate the dynamic group discourse among teachers of different subjects, different learning backgrounds, and different social status. The teachers of the general school subjects were all university graduates (with first or second degrees), whereas the teachers of the vocational subjects had no academic background. Yet, here in the group, the academic teachers admit their failure compared to their non-academic colleagues. The latter seem to have made their subject matter much more meaningful and, therefore, more appealing to the students.

Success was seen in the group, both in affective terms, in their sense of responsibility, independence and joy, and in cognitive terms. Namely, in higher-order learning operations, oscillating between the concrete and the abstract by discriminating between the symbol and the object by translating a design into a concrete product. This led one of the teachers to offer a new definition for *significant or meaningful learning*.

- Individual work, with very clear objectives and a concrete track of action, that engages body and soul. The movement of the material is in rhythm with that of the learner. It is also creative in the sense of producing a valuable product...

From the general theoretical level, the group moved on to the applicative level; how to turn their new learning into improved teaching. The question here is, "How can the process be analyzed into its different components, differentiating the 'tools' from the specific 'contents' thereby adapting the tools into new learning contexts?"

One indication of such a 'transfer' was the joint math and mechanics curriculum unit, which the teachers subsequently developed and implemented experimentally. The idea of integrating two subject matters, which had already been raised, became much more feasible once the math teacher raised the need to change the conventional curriculum orientation. Developing a curriculum unit that would stem from the basic requirements of the mechanics subject matter and integrate math as a necessary formal thinking tool for calculations would be likely to enhance 'mathematical thinking' and lead to an interplay between theory and practice.

Moral Education or Education of Values

Learning ability represented only one of the areas that the group sought to improve. The other source of discontent, voiced at the beginning of the process, was how to deal with issues related to values and norms in education. Discussion of this aspect of teaching was not planned; it emerged on the group's agenda as a result of unforeseen classroom events.

The first circumstantial incident, which took place at the beginning of the year, was an act of vandalism involving the breaking windows and furniture in this particular classroom. Ricky, the home-teacher, decided to raise the matter in one of the regular group meetings in order to sound the group on the question of punishment. The discussion that followed highlighted two different themes or principles: (a) that the students should take the responsibility for the repair work, and (b) that as a punishment, they would have to cover the costs.

However, no decision was taken. Ricky said she needed more time to think and the group seemed reluctant to elaborate on the subject. Was this an indication of the group's immaturity? It seemed as if they were not ready at this early stage to turn disciplinary events into learning opportunities, which could help resolve a problem they themselves had identified.

Two months later, dramatic reports of classroom theft forced them to postpone all other issues and focus on this particular turn of events, which, in turn, led to discussion of issues surrounding educational norms and values. This development called for a change in our mode of group-work; which had been largely based on classroom observations. I decided to apply the 'Heuristic-model for problem solving' (see Chapter 2), which seemed appropriate for dealing with this issue. The six stages of the model were as follows:

(1) identifying the area of discontent;
(2) formulating a research question;
(3) data collection;
(4) diagnosing the basic problem;
(5) generating working hypotheses, ways of treatment, as proposals for further experimentation, and finally
(6) reflection and self-evaluation of the process.

In the following, is a brief description of the problem-solving process in the group:

Formulating a research question: How do we cope with cases of lawbreaking, in general, and with thefts, in particular? Is it part of our role as teachers of this particular class?

Data collection: All of the teachers had some information about the phenomenon but it was only after a systematic round of reports in the group that a fuller picture unfolded. This particular class had a long history of thefts. On the other hand, a new girl with a story of past thefts had just been admitted to the class for a probationary period. Information gathered from parents highlighted another aspect: It seemed that the students had a good idea as who the suspects were but felt reluctant to 'tell on them'.

Diagnosing the basic problem is recognized as the most difficult stage of the process. It requires liberation from participants' tunnel vision (Miller 1982) of the situation. The first automatic solution of our teachers was to summon the police; in other words, to throw the responsibility onto external agents instead of taking it upon themselves. Finally, they were able to generate two working questions: (1) How to deal with the suspects, and (2) How to deal with the phenomenon of theft, which, in Israeli society, is coupled with the norm of 'social solidarity'.

Once this second question was explicitly formulated, the group realized that the real problem we faced was that of conflicting educational values. Moreover, the incident provided the group with an optimal opportunity to deal with the immanent difficulty of having to choose between two positive values, truth versus social solidarity. This example opened the participants' eyes to opportunities for 'value education' contained in real events in the everyday life of the classroom.

Generating working hypotheses, ways of treatment: Two working hypotheses were formulated: (a) The two suspect girls will be handled separately (by the head teacher of the 10th grade), and (b) The issue of conflicting values will be discussed seriously in a special classroom activity conducted by Ricky, their home teacher.

The prior feeling of reluctance expressed earlier in the group now gave way to a strong feeling of responsibility, suggesting that the case should be further elaborated by each teacher within the framework of his or her subject area.

It so happened that the next group meeting took place immediately after the learning process led by Janet the Scriptures teacher. It is thus not surprising that the question of values became an important issue and a learning objective. It also paved the way for several teachers to relate to the issue of values within their own classroom activities.

Reflection and self-evaluation of the process: Although the actual phenomenon of theft disappeared, participants felt the need to evaluate the group problem-solving process and the impact of their decision to act. The teachers, who continued practicing 'value education' within their respective subject areas, were asked to recount their experiences. The following excerpt is taken from the next group discourse:

Scripture teacher: - They arrived at the conclusion that society interferes with the individual and so I asked them how do we escape such situations? We elaborated on the subject in conjunction with the Psalm that we were studying as well as with the matter of the thefts. I emphasized that I was acquainted with the facts, hoping that they would get the message and that A. would confess, which, in fact, she did, eventually.

Hebrew literature teacher: - I chose particular texts that would trigger them to relate to their personal problems. I am always trying to find texts that are relevant to their everyday lives and that is what I did with respect to the issue of the thefts.

Gila, the 10th grade head teacher, whose responsibility was to implement the group decision with respect to the two suspect girls, recounted her side of the story:

Head teacher: - After gathering information from the different perspectives expressed in the group, I realized there was evidence confirming my suspicions. The picture cleared up and I felt I could handle the case.... The group message was clearly to act and not just carry on... Today, I am quite certain that we were too considerate in dealing with the previous case of window breaking. This was interpreted by students as weakness and, hence, paved the way to more vandalism. I see the great advantage of our group work, in terms of decision-making, which guided me, supported me, while actually requiring me to do the dirty work... Once the decision was taken, I turned it into a 'case'. I summoned the girls and asked them to tell me what had happened. They confessed to it all. My next step was to manipulate between two norms: the first, that students cannot be expelled from school before the end of the year, and the second, that failure or a grade of 'unsatisfactory' for conduct is a formal reason for expulsion. I elaborated on the point that given an unsatisfactory grade for conduct, I could report to the inspector and start the procedure for their expulsion. Yet, sensing some signs of repentance on their side, and first buds of communication between us, I suggested we suspend their unsatisfactory grade, leaving them on probation until the end of the year. Their part of the bargain was to make sure that I receive only positive reports about their conduct until then. They had to hand in their locker keys, which meant carrying their kit every day from home to school and back again. But they kept the deal and by the end of the year, the unsatisfactory conduct grade was cancelled.

In conclusion, I would like to share some of my thinking with you and highlight a few points, which, to me, summarize the important role played by the group: First and foremost, clarifying the picture by looking at it from different facets; second, making a decision about a path of action, and, finally, supporting me, as the person who had to implement the decision. How to act was my own decision and, believe me, I make a lot of decisions. However, this time I felt secure. I was acting on behalf of the group's general consensus, and also, I felt I was acting in a more professional, less intuitive way.

To assess the educational impact on the class of our dealing with the problem of value education in this particular case, we needed to collect data from the students. It was decided in the group that I, as the only non-teaching person in the group, would interview four students, to be chosen by Ricky. The interview was recorded and played back in the next group meeting.

The reaction was devastating. Although most participants were able to point to important and valuable information in terms of exposing the students' point of reference, some rather unpleasant notes were voiced in the discussion, such as:

- Itt reminds me of Orwell's 1984... of children informing on their parents.
- I am disturbed by having one-sided information, information about the teacher that is not balanced by his or her point of view...
- The problem I see is how to deal with conflicting interests. It is important to get the student's side of the story but it violates the teacher's basic human rights...

The incident was referred to as the 'explosion', thus revealing the vulnerability of the participants, their fluctuation between open-minded tolerance and critical reflection, and defensive mechanisms, laden with suspicion and basic fears. The ethical issue as well as the connotations of Orwell's 1984 revealed the difficulty of teachers to accept feedback from their students. It seemed that they had forgotten their own objective, which was to gain insight into the impact of their intentional actions. Their rational decisions were replaced by the primordial fear of a 'big brother'.

Figure 3.1 provides a graphic representation of the group work during the year. The cyclic process of learning in the group based on classroom observation is on the left side. On the right are the instances taken from the classroom reality, which were picked up by the group as opportunities for learning. This is the reason for placing the Scripture lesson in a central position, as a junction for the two different problems that were dealt with in the group, a medium for the two modes of group work. The 'explosion' as part of the process of dealing with values in education, actually created a new ethical question: "Is it ethical to use student feedback information on their teachers?" This remains an open question.

Discussion

The case study presented above, which could be seen as another example of our work within the framework of institutional learning or school-renewal, clearly has a different focus. By turning my attention from the macro- to the micro-level, my intention was to gain deeper insight into the process of teachers' professional development in a reflective group. I shall start by reviewing our group work from two different perspectives – the context and the process – and discussing the nature of the group and the process of teachers' learning.

Our group, consisting of 10 teachers, each representing a different subject area, can be seen as a representative sample of the comprehensive school teaching staff. As already mentioned (see Chapter 2), the vocational and academic teachers represent two different socio-educational groups. Yet, 'compartmentalization' goes far beyond this classification, reflecting a subtle hierarchy of subject matters. On entering the staff room of any high school, one cannot fail to notice the way teachers cluster in subject groups. Hierarchically, the math teachers are at the top of the ladder. In this particular school they have their own table in the staff room around which no other teacher dares to sit even when the place is vacant. Next in rank come the Sciences, English as a second language, and further down, the Humanities.

The vocational teachers, at the bottom of the social ladder, have their own subtle hierarchy between technological subjects and home economics, sewing and child-care.

This hierarchy was reflected in the group at the beginning of our joint work, creating a non-egalitarian climate. Moreover, the academic teachers, whose main role is to teach the 'clever students' in the top classes, were reluctant to teach low-achieving classes, such as the class forming the focus of our story. Their patronizing attitudes are heard in the discourse (for example, when the math teacher comments on Ricky's low level teaching).

The change in climate can be sensed already in the second cycle of learning. Notwithstanding the fact that Janet is a novice teacher and Scripture is considered a rather low ranking subject, observing her teaching leads to more egalitarian attitudes. An atmosphere of equality gradually develops between the participants of different social status.

This trend is very pronounced in the fourth learning cycle, where the academic teachers of prestigious subjects give full credit to their vocational colleagues. They applaud their success in areas in which they themselves have totally failed, such as reaching out to their students and motivating their learning. As a result, not only do they raise the self-esteem of the vocational teachers but they also contribute towards establishing a more egalitarian social climate among the staff. I consider an egalitarian social school climate to be a very important factor in the school culture, as well as being in line with the underlying rationale of the comprehensive school.

It is interesting to note that Gila, the head teacher of the 10th grade, whose position within the school hierarchy is high, is quick to sense and appreciate this change of climate. She is able to define the difference between having the support of the group in the decision-making process and between having to make a decision herself.

Figure 3.1: A graphic representation of group work

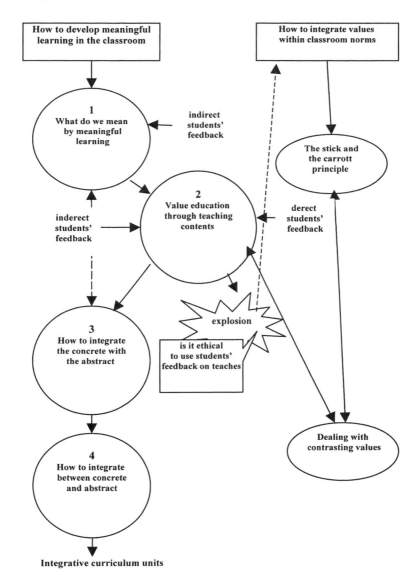

I believe that maintaining an egalitarian relationship between participants of different status is a prerequisite for an effective reflective group, as well as for peer learning. However, it should be emphasized that the egalitarian nature of a group is not achieved by overlooking the differences, or pretending they do not exist. It is based on acknowledgment and acceptance of the differences between members. It requires the facilitator's change of role conception, the change of the 'time' concept or that of the group efficiency. His or her first priority is to develop a reflective group before any other aims or 'products' of the process can be achieved. Only when participants feel they are on equal ground does the group become a reflective group that can function as a 'hall of mirrors'– a reflective group that reflects many diverse aspects of a situation, such as an observed lesson. As mirrors, each participant reflects his or her unique conceptions, perspectives, or reference points. For such a multifaceted reflection to occur, participants have to feel safe and not threatened by their peers' judgments.

The learning process in the group, which was actually initiated by the teachers, was basically action-research oriented. Except for Gila, the head teacher of the 10th grade, I do not recall any of them participating in action-research settings before. I served as a trigger only insofar as I required them to generate questions, thus setting them within an inquiry framework. Ricky's suggestion to invite the group to observe her classroom teaching was no less a surprise for me. I saw it as indication of her professional confidence combined with a real desire to investigate the puzzling situation that she was facing. The first group discussion following the observation illustrates the participants' first steps in 'reflection-on-action'. They start cautiously, first praising and then gradually moving on to problematic issues; for example, reflecting on her summary sheet, from the point of view of myself as a student. This is a completely different approach to that of the more common type of feedback voiced by inspectors or other higher-rank teachers. The multifaceted comments balance each other, minimizing the judgment effect. The only way to elicit evidence of the effectiveness of the process is to follow the excerpts and probe deeper and deeper into the teaching/learning situations.

Naturally, we all (teachers and researchers) learned as we proceeded, making every new cycle more significant and meaningful in terms of learning about teaching and learning about learning.

How to integrate educational and pedagogical theories with the teachers' practical knowledge is a perennial issue on the agenda of teacher education. Teachers' reluctance to learn from the research literature is a known fact, which I believe indicates their notion of theoretical knowledge as non-relevant and a separate entity from their practice. Our group work challenged these attitudes by introducing relevant reading material as part of the cycle of learning. The participant teachers, after reporting on the different papers they had read, were able to relate the theories to the actual issues discussed in the group. This was not an immediate effect. Only gradually, as new knowledge was reconstructed did more and more theoretical concepts appear in the discourse. This also triggered more reading, making it a more meaningful way of learning and, hopefully, changing their prior antagonism towards the research literature.

The main product of the group process was to construct new professional knowledge in other words, to trigger the participants to conceptualize their practice, their teaching/learning experiences into theories-of-action. The interplay between practice and theory is enhanced by the dialectical process of reflection in the group. This stands in contrast to the separation of theory from practice, separation between the abstract and the concrete, which characterizes prevailing notions of knowledge. Our alternative concept of construction and reconstruction of professional knowledge, involves moving from the practice to a theory-of-action and back again to test this new theory in the classroom.

This interplay between the concrete and the theoretical is even more enhanced in a heterogeneous setting, such as our group; for example, in the mechanical workshop, where the students' learning was conceived in terms of an interplay between the two-dimensional design of the object and the three-dimensional created object. The idea of an integrative curriculum also stemmed from this new understanding of the workshop; a curriculum unit that integrates sewing with geography around the common key concept of 'scale', and a module aimed at developing 'mathematical thinking' by integrating concrete mechanics with math.

I close this chapter by quoting the group's new definition of – meaningful learning': " (it) engages body and soul. The movement of the material is in rhythm with that of the learner..."

I believe that a process that engages body and soul also integrates *'learning with living'*, pulling down the artificial boundaries between school knowledge and life knowledge. In terms of the teachers, it implies removal of the boundary between teachers' professional development and their personal growth.

Chapter 4

School Evaluation as a Dialogue between Teachers and Researchers[1]

The process of school renewal in which we were engaged can also be seen as a process of school self-evaluation, where self-evaluation is initiated and implemented by the school with the aim of serving the school's internal aims (Lewy 1989). There seems to be a contradiction between the idea of self-evaluation and that of external intervention. I will argue that the appearance or non-appearance of such a contradiction is related to the definition of self-evaluation and on the type of partnership that develops between the staff of the school and the researchers.

The ability of the school to carry out self-evaluation, that is, to assess the adequacy and efficacy of its own decisions and its skill in implementing them, is an indicator of the autonomy of the school (Reshef 1989). We worked with Lewy's (1989) view of self-evaluation as a process, which is initiated and implemented by the school staff, the results of which provide an answer to the school's internal aims and not those of external agencies.

In the case described here, the school is a large comprehensive school in the south of Israel. Our partnership had begun a few years earlier in the framework of a school self-renewal project (reported in Chapter 2). A new principal had entered the scene and had taken the initiative of forming a 'management group' in order to introduce 'second-order change' in the school.

The problem identified by this newly formed group was how to improve the school image in the eyes of its clients or how to make the school more attractive and meaningful for its students. Facilitated by me, we met regularly for a whole year, indulging in a process of inquiry, collecting data from the field as well as from the research literature. Our 'diagnosis' suggested that instead of constituting one integrated institution of learning, the comprehensive school, in actual fact, functions like two separate entities: one with an academic orientation and the other with a vocational-technical orientation, with little social integration between them. This led to the decision to experiment 'unstreaming' or mixed ability teaching (MAT). After experimenting with MAT for two years with our cooperative assistance, the management of the school asked us to assist them in its evaluation.

An evaluation report had to be submitted to the Ministry of Education, who had financed the evaluation project. We decided that the report would serve not only as 'product' or tool for decision-making, but also as a means for self-evaluation. We wanted to turn the process of evaluation into an opportunity for self-reflection and organizational learning.

Thus, the topic of evaluation was Mixed Ability Teaching (MAT), which had been implemented as a means of enhancing social integration. In order to avoid the potential contradiction between self-evaluation and the intervention of researchers in the partnership, it was important for us to be 'user-focused' in every possible sense (House 1978). We could not impose decisions. The partnership had to take the form of a 'reflective dialogue' between us the researchers and the staff of the school as an autonomous self-evaluating body (Clandinin 1985, Wilson, Shulman and Richert 1987, Elliott 1989, Richardson 1990, Gore and Zeichner 1991). A reflexive dialogue between researchers and practitioners is a type of interaction, which enables the practitioners to modify their perception of situations and reframe their knowledge (Schon 1983). The partners in the dialogue, namely the researchers and the practitioners, are not necessarily equal: The teachers are usually far more knowledgeable about the practice of teaching. Confronted daily with the shortcomings of current teaching methods, they are the ones who actually carry out the decisions concerning the selection and implementation of new methods.   Researchers, on the other hand, are more knowledgeable as to the theoretical aspects of education and educational evaluation (Elbaz 1981).   However, it is worth mentioning that quite often, as in our case, theoretical knowledge is not strictly 'neutral': It often reflects educational ideas and approaches, about what, the researchers' believe should actually be done in the classroom.

A reflective dialogue in such a context involves a process of interaction, which can take place only between partners whose contributions are truly complementary. Two essential conditions have to be fulfilled:

(a) The practitioners, having experienced the new methods, need to be provided with a basis for the dialogue, that is, factual, empirical data.
(b) The researchers, as well as the practitioners, have to become sensitized to their own perceptions and to their interlocutors' perceptions of the questions to be asked and the problems to be solved.

Our aim here is not to assess the success or failure of the MAT project but to describe the *patterns* of evaluation which provided the necessary types of empirical results and to show how the various outcomes were integrated into a final report.

The Evaluative Scheme and the Involvement of the Researchers

Based on the questions raised by the school staff, three areas of evaluation were delineated:

(1) student achievement;
(2) classroom climate, and
(3) teachers' behavior in MAT classes.

The need for evaluation on all three parameters was recognized by the practitioners but the involvement of the researchers differed in each case.

In the case of student achievement, the instruments of evaluation were developed and administered by the teachers who also assessed the performance of the students. We became involved only at the stage of the *interpretation* of results. In the case of classroom climate, we became involved already in the early stage of *selection of the instru-ments*. The issue itself was raised by the teachers, who considered the social climate to be a direct indicator of social integration. However, the decision to use the LEI questionnaire (Hofstein, Ben-Zvi and Carmeli 1990, see below) was consistent with our wider assumptions ('unequal partners') concerning the link between social integration, effective Mixed-Ability (MA) teaching and the classroom climate as the learning environment (Keiny and Dreyfus 1989).

The last issue, teachers' behavior in MAT classes, differed from the others in the sense that it had been raised by the school management and not by the teachers. The school management wanted to know if MAT had brought about a substantial change in teaching strategies. Their request concurred with our need to validate MAT. However, they had no defined hypothesis and so we were actually involved in all the stages of this part of the evaluation.

The Target Population: Non-Streamed, Mixed-Ability Classes

The comprehensive high school of the type referred to here consists of 9th to 12th grade (ages 15 to 18) students. In this school, there were ten 9th grade and ten 10th grade classes divided into three main streams: (1) the top level 'Academic' stream in which the scholastic ability and achievement level was equivalent to that of regular academic high schools; (2) the lowest level 'Practical' or 'Vocational' stream consisting of students evaluated as unable to meet the matriculation exam requirements and not normally expected to move upwards to a higher stream, and (3) the intermediate 'Comprehensive' stream consisting of students expected to take and pass at least part of the matriculation examinations (using a curriculum with a technological rather than academic slant). The three streams correspond to the three Math sets, mentioned in Chapter2.

The MAT experiment was implemented in the 9th and 10th grades only. The heterogeneous non-streamed (MA) experimental classes were selected from the 'academic' and 'comprehensive' streams in the following way: Each 9th and 10th grade class was divided randomly into three equal parts, three 'thirds'. Then two academic 'thirds' originating from different classes were combined with one comprehensive 'third', thus producing a heterogeneous class with about one-third of the students from the comprehensive stream. Eight 9th grade classes were thus obtained, with a total of 306 students (100 comprehensive and 206 academic), and six 10th grade classes (226 students, 68 comprehensive and 158 academic).

Only two subjects were included in the experiment: Scripture and History (compulsory subjects at all the levels of Israeli education). Because both of these subjects were scheduled for three weekly hours, the hetererogeneous non-streamed classes met for only six periods each week. Ten History and seven Scripture teachers took part in the experiment.

The Instruments and Patterns of Evaluation

(a) Classroom Achievement

No special instrument was designed to assess the achievements of individual students in the two settings. Two types of 'routine' instrument were used, 'classroom marks' represented by the grades in the trimester reports, and 'criterion scores' obtained from 'criterion exams' prepared centrally and taken simultaneously by all students in the same grade. Students' achievements were assessed at the end of the third trimester according to the following design:

(1) Scores obtained in non-streamed (MA) settings were compared with scores obtained by the same students in their original homogeneous classes. Obviously, such a comparison could not be made simply on the basis of the same subject matter

because the experimental groups studied *only* Scripture and History in non-streamed (MA) settings, and because they studied these subjects *only* in such settings. So, scores for Scripture and History were compared with those obtained in two subjects taught only in the original homogeneous classes, namely, Math and Geography. Math was selected as representing a difficult subject matter and Geography because it was surmised that its level of difficulty is more or less equivalent to that of History and Scripture.

(2) Classroom scores in Scripture and History were compared with the criterion scores obtained by the same students.

(b) The Learning Environment Inventory (LEI)

Developed and validated in connection with the Harvard Physics Project, the LEI has been shown to be a sensitive instrument for measuring students' perceptions of the classroom social learning climate (Walberg and Anderson 1968, Anderson 1973). A modified Hebrew version was tested and adjusted to Israeli conditions by Hofstein, Gluzman, Ben-Zvi and Samuel (1990), who also showed that each of its various scales can be used independently.

Eight LEI scales (named and defined according to Anderson, 1973) were used in this study, namely, Speed, Friction, Goal orientation, Democracy, Favoritism, Satisfaction, Competitiveness, and Difficulty (see Appendix 1 for definitions). The LEI Inventory measures each variable separately on a four-point scale. The teachers' score for each variable consists of the mean class score obtained on the items of the relevant scale. The LEI is not designed to assess the general climate prevailing in the classroom; it was designed to measure the climate created *in a given class by a particular teacher* while teaching *a specific subject matter*. The mean scores of the various scales produce a 'profile' reflecting the behavior of the teacher as perceived by the students.

According to the approach of this study, a desirable profile would consist of a high score on goal orientation, democracy, and satisfaction, a low score on friction, favoritism and competitiveness. Extreme scores on speed and difficulty are seen as undesirable. Because some scales are regarded as positive and others as negative, a desirable profile is characterized by a wide amplitude (positive traits high, and negative traits low) (see experimental group in Figure 4.1).

In our experiment, the students were not aware of either the definition or the existence of the eight scales. The LEI questionnaires were administered by research students, twice in each class: the first time, in the MA (History or Scripture experimental setting) class, and the second time, in the Hebrew Language or Hebrew Literature lessons (two compulsory subjects taught in the regular homogeneous classes serving as a control). In this way, two different class-perceptions were obtained for the same group of students.

(c) Classroom Observations

The observers were given an observation sheet focusing on the following, characteristics of teaching behavior (see Appendix 2):

(1) Amount of teacher talk.
(2) Types of teacher question.
(3) Number of student questions.
(4) Time devoted to various types of discussion.
(5) Time devoted to types of task in which the students were actively involved.
(6) Teacher response to student initiatives.
(7) Types of teacher intervention during sessions of active learning

Thus, it can be seen that our observation system dealt with specific categories of behavior seen as relevant to MAT. The outcomes of the observations enabled us to focus on the tendencies of the teacher (a) to design differential learning assignments (i.e., to try to adapt different tasks to the abilities and motivations of different students); (b) to be sensitive to the behavior of the students and attentive to their classroom behavior and performance, and (c) to encourage students to assume responsibility for their learning.

Figure 4.1: **Mean LEI profiles of the experimental and the control   groups.**

Legend: SP=Speed; FR=Friction; GO=Goal Orientation;
        DE=Democracy; DI=Difficulty; FA=Favouritism;
        SA=Satisfaction; CO=Competitiveness

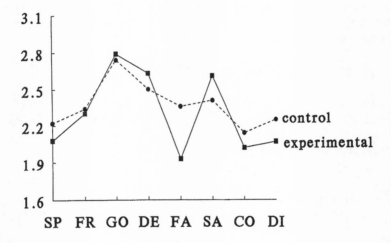

The observers wrote down a full script of the observed lessons and identified relevant events in terms of the above-mentioned categories. The categories were straightforward and we found that they presented no difficulty for the observers with regard to either identification or inter-observer agreement.

Main Findings

(a) Classroom Achievement

The school was keen to obtain an answer to two main questions:

(1) Did comprehensive students gain or suffer from being taught in the heterogeneous (MA) settings? (For example, were the scores obtained by comprehensive students in non-streamed settings low because they were assessed according to 'academic' standards?)

(2) Did the academic students gain or suffer from being taught in MA settings? (For example, were the standards of achievement lowered due to their adaptation to the abilities of the weaker students?)

It can be seen that the criteria for 'suffering' with regard to comprehensive students (inability to cope with standards) differed from those used for 'academic' students (lowering of the standards). The 'classroom' scores obtained by academic students in heterogeneous settings were, therefore, compared with the scores obtained by the same students in homogeneous (MA) settings in order to assess the academic level in the MA classes. The same comparison, regarding comprehensive students, was used as an indication of their ability to cope with the level of the MA.

As the results for 9th and 10th grade were similar, for reasons of space, only those of the 9th grade will be reported.

The average scores of the comprehensive students in MA classes (Scripture and History) were systematically (in all the classes) and significantly lower than their classroom scores obtained in homo-geneous settings (Geography and Math) by an average of 10 and 5 marks out of a maximum of 100, respectively. There was, however, no systematic difference (average of less than 0.5 mark) between the corresponding results of the academic students. The conclusion appeared to be straightforward: In heterogeneous settings, students were judged according to standard academic criteria and in the homo-geneous classes, according to the expected level of the class. As far as the academic students were concerned, this made no difference, but the comprehensive population appeared to have 'suffered' from being taught in heterogeneous settings. *These findings indicated that in the MA settings, the standard of teaching was comparable to that of the academic stream.*

To assess the ability of the comprehensive students to survive in heterogeneous settings, the average classroom scores of the compre-hensive students in Scripture and History were compared with their average 'criterion' scores: The classroom scores were, on average, 15 marks higher than the corresponding criterion examination scores, and in History, the average difference was even greater: about 20 marks. The criterion examination (assessed according to uniform *academic* standards) appeared, therefore, to be unfavorable to the comprehensive students. The same comparison yielded smaller differences for the academic population (about 9 and 6 marks higher, respectively).

These were the main results – in 'black and white' – and this is where we decided to intervene. The overall results could hardly be denied. The question was whether a different picture emerges when the results are analyzed on the basis of individual students or individual teachers.

The individual criterion test scores of 38 percent of the comprehensive students in History and 24 percent in Scripture were *found to be equal to or above the average* of the heterogeneous class on the same test. The corresponding percentages for (MA) classroom scores were 24 percent and 25 percent, respectively. Although these results do not contradict the overall statistical picture, they show that between one-fourth and one-third of the comprehensive students had actually *'gained'* by *academic* standards. Because the main objective of the criterion examination was to rank the students and/or the classes by means of an external criterion, standard scores were computed for both types of test.

The general tendency of the results obtained with standard scores indicated that students *neither gained nor lost* from being taught in heterogeneous settings; their classroom *ranking* tended to correspond to their objective criterion test ranking. However, when scores were checked *on the basis of individual teachers*, deviations from the general tendency were found. Comparison of the six Scripture teachers revealed that for one of them, the average classroom standard score was 0.58 lower than the corresponding criterion standard scores, for another teacher, the difference was 0.25, and for a third teacher, an opposite trend was found (classroom scores 0.23 higher than criterion scores). The remaining three teachers were remarkably accurate in their scoring, with only negligible differences; this was also true for three of the History teachers. Thus, the academic standards required by some teachers appeared to be higher than those required by the criterion test and in one case, they were lower. Other teachers, on the other hand, appeared to be 'well-tuned'.

Could these tendencies of the teachers be related to other characteristics to be uncovered by the other instruments of evaluation?

(b) Classroom Climate (LEI)

The climate in the classroom was assessed by the students in all 14 MA classes (History and Scripture, N=393). Six Hebrew Literature teachers, who taught the *same* students in the regular homogeneous settings, formed the control group. Figure 4.1 shows the mean profiles of the experimental and control groups. It can be seen that the learning environment of the experimental (MA) group was perceived as markedly

(a) more satisfactory,
(b) more democratic,
(c) less difficult, and
(d) more egalitarian (less favoritism) than that of the control group.

However, we were more interested in the behavior of individual teachers of the experimental group than in group averages.

Table 4.1 presents the LEI scores of 13 of the experimenting teachers (6 Scripture, 7 History). The Scripture teachers formed an apparently homogeneous group: A positive classroom climate was observed with high scores on satisfaction and democracy and relatively low scores on favoritism and difficulty. The range of behaviors was wider in the History group, where some teachers obtained lower scores on goal orientation, democracy and satisfaction, and scored higher on favoritism and difficulty. The shape of the profile curves provide a fairly accurate illustration of the differences in classroom climate.

Because the desirable behavior of MA teachers was characterized by high scores on three scales (goal orientation, democracy, and satisfaction) and lower scores on the remaining five, the 'amplitude' of the curve was an indicator of the degree of adaptation of the teachers to the recommended strategies.(see Figure 4.2)

Teachers who had not truly adopted these strategies yielded rather 'flat' profiles. For instance, from Figure 4.2, which shows the individual profiles of three Scripture and three History teachers together with the mean profile of the experimental group, it is clear that the 'amplitude' of the curves of teachers 4 and 18 is markedly larger than average and that teacher 15 yielded a rather 'flat' profile.

(c) Classroom Observations

Two specially trained observers observed six teachers, each for five periods during the year. Using the observation sheet, each category-defined event was recorded and when relevant, its length (in minutes) was measured. The observers also produced a detailed description of the lessons. For reasons of space, and because our aim here is only to describe patterns of evaluation, we shall discuss here only three characteristic teachers whose profiles are represented in Figure 4.2.

Figure 4.2 The LEI profiles (broken lines) of three
Scripture and   three History teachers,
compared to the mean profile of the
experimental group (unbroken lines).

Legend: SP=Speed; FR=Friction; GO=Goal Orientation;
DE=Democracy; FA=Favouritism; SA=Satisfaction;
CO=Competitiveness; DI=Difficulty.

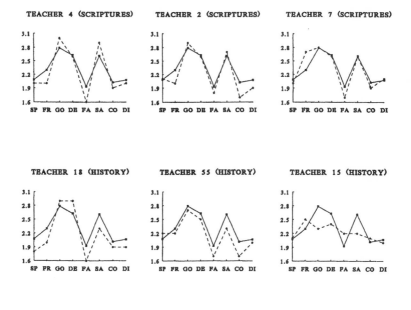

Table 4.l: Mean LEI Scores (in brackets: standard deviations) of the Scripture and History Teachers

Scripture teachers

Teacher (by number)	2	3	4	5	6	7
	(n=60)	(n=31)	(n=28)	(n=28)	(n=24)	(n=34)
Speed	2.1(.3)	1.8(.3)	2.0(.4)	2.2(.4)	2.0(.4)	2.0(.6)
Friction	2.0(.4)	2.1(.5)	2.0(.5)	2.6(.5)	2.0(.5)	2.7(.5)
Goal-orientation	2.9(.3)	2.9(.4)	3.0(.5)	2.7(.4)	2.7(.4)	2.8(.5)
Democracy	2.6(.3)	2.7(.3)	2.6(.3)	2.8(.4)	2.5(.3)	2.6(.3)
Favoritism	1.8(.6)	1.8(.6)	1.6(.5)	2.1(.5)	2.0(.7)	1.7(.7)
Satisfaction	2.7(.4)	2.8(.4)	2.9(.5)	2.7(.4)	2.6(.6)	2.6(.6)
Comprtitiveness	1.7(.5)	2.1(.7)	1.9(.7)	2.2(.4)	2.1(.6)	1.9(.5)
Difficulty	1.9(.5)	2.0(.5)	2.0(.4)	1.9(.5)	2.0(.5)	2.1(.5)

History teachers

Teacher (by number)	11	12	13	15	18	19	55
	(n=32)	(n=27)	(n=25)	(n=23)	(n=29)	(n=26)	(n=30)
Speed	2.0(.2)	2.3(.5)	2.1(.4)	2.1(.4)	1.8(.4)	2.0(.3)	2.2(.5)
Friction	2.2(.4)	2.6(.5)	2.2(.4)	2.5(.5)	2.0(.3)	2.2(.5)	2.2(.5)
Goal-orientation	2.9(.4)	2.5(.5)	2.9(.3)	2.3(.6)	2.9(.3)	2.0(.5)	2.7(.6)
Democracy	2.5(.3)	2.4(.4)	2.5(.2)	2.4(.3)	2.9(.3)	2.7(.4)	2.5(.3)
Favoritism	1.8(.5)	2.2(.7)	1.7(.4)	2.2(.5)	1.6(.6)	2.1(.7)	1.7(.5)
Satisfaction	2.2(.5)	2.2(.6)	2.6(.4)	2.2(.6)	2.3(.4)	2.0(.4)	2.3(.4)
Competi-tiveness	2.0(.5)	2.2(.8)	2.0(.4)	2.1(.7)	1.9(.5)	1.8(.4)	1.7(.5)
Difficulty	2.1(.3)	2.3(.4)	2.1(.3)	2.0(.6)	1.9(.4)	1.9(.5)	2.0(.5)

Teacher 2: Osnat (Scripture)

Osnat's tactics remained stable throughout all of the five observed periods. She opened the lesson by reading out verses from the Bible (6-7 minutes' teacher talk). This category did not decrease during the year, nor did the number of 'closed' questions which served, 'ping-pong' style, to check students' homework.   However, her tendency to adapt her teaching to individual students was observed to increase according to several criteria: open questions (from 1 to 5), rephrased questions (from 1 to 6). A tangible change was recorded in the time she allotted in each period to independent learning assignments (from 0 minutes in the first period to 5, 24, 37, and 29 minutes in the periods that followed).   Her attentiveness to student-initiated questions was high from the beginning, and in two different cases in the last lessons, she was observed responding to non-verbal cues of students. In both cases, she gave the class a short assignment and was thus able to devote some time to these individual students.

Teacher 4: Sarit (Scripture)

Sarit's teaching behavior evolved continuously from one observation to the next. The amount of teacher talk decreased (from 7 minutes to 12, 0, 4, 3 minutes, respectively), and so did the number of closed questions (from 14 to 5). The number of open questions increased (from 3 to 5), as well as the number of rephrased questions (from 2 to 7) and student-initiated questions (from 4 to 8). Two out of the five observed lessons consisted mainly of group work. The groups were heterogeneous, each member being responsible for a personal contribution to the group task. Cooperative learning was recorded in most groups. She responded patiently to all students who sought her assistance, directing them to their group or to other sources of knowledge rather than supplying the answer herself.

Teacher 15: Bat-Sheva (History)

Very little change was recorded in Bat-Sheva's teaching behavior. Her lessons were of the teacher-centered, 'frontal' type. Teacher talk scored high (5, 4, 15, 5 minutes), and so did the number of closed questions (9, 7, 7, 15, 7). No open questions were recorded in four of the five observed periods. The number of rephrased questions decreased (16 and 11 in the two first lessons to 1 and 3 in the two last lessons). Student-initiated questions (1, 1, 2, 5, 1) were only partially answered. A different pattern was observed in the fourth period; assignments were given and the students worked in pairs. However, the aspect of independent learning was minimized by the behavior of Bat-Sheva, who supplied the right answer immediately in response to all student questions.

To sum-up: Osnat, who was attentive to her students from the beginning, improved her questioning (in the desired direction) and devoted more time to individual/independent student learning. Sarit (a novice teacher) showed a distinctive change in her teaching style, from teacher-centered to more student-oriented. Bat-Sheva's dominant teacher-centered behavior remained unchanged throughout the year, and was unaffected by the MA setting.

All of the findings yielded by the three methods of evaluation (achievement, LEI, and observation) were reported to the school management, thus providing the 'hard' data needed for decision-making. However, we saw it as our task to interpret this data in a way that would make sense, that is, provide useful answers to the school's original questions: *Did MAT bring about better social integration of the 'comprehensive' population without lowering the scholastic achievement of the 'academic' students*?

Making Sense of the Findings

The overall outcomes were not clear-cut because it seemed that some teachers adapted themselves better than others to the demands and philosophy of MAT. By emphasizing the individual outcomes, we could shift from the school's basic hypothesis

(MAT brings about social integration) to a more refined set of hypotheses:

a) Certain specific teacher behaviors enhance successful MAT.
b) MAT improves the learning achievement of a substantial part of the comprehensive population.
c) The climate in successful MA classes is conducive to social integration.

To illustrate this point, let us combine the outcomes of teachers 2, 4, and 15 on each of the evaluation tools, as presented above, into a meaningful set of interrelated characteristics.

Osnat: Osnat taught Scripture in two different MAT settings (i.e., in six 'thirds,' two of them comprehensive and four academic). The differences between her average classroom standard scores and the corresponding criterion standard scores were negligible for all the groups (range from 0.02 to -0.2 SD). Her LEI scores revealed a positive classroom climate, as shown by high scores on goal orientation, student satisfaction and democracy, and low scores on friction, competitiveness and favoritism (see Figure 4.2, teacher2).
She was (observations) very attentive to her students' questions and sensitive to their need for help. The evolution of her teaching behavior was characterized by an increase in behaviors that enhance independent student learning (open and rephrased questions, independent learning assignments). Osnat appeared to be a 'reflective teacher.' She quickly realized that conventional teaching did not meet the demands of MAT and, therefore, she adjusted her teaching behavior so as to be able to cope with the heterogeneity of her classes.   As a result, the 'standard' achievement level in her classes, as explained in a previous section, showed that, on the one hand, there was *no discrimination of the comprehensive students* and, on the other, the performance of all of the students was judged according to stable 'academic' standards.

Sarit: The picture obtained for this young beginner teacher was, to some extent, similar to that obtained for Osnat.   The differences between average classroom standard scores and the corresponding criterion standard scores were negligible, ranging from SD=0 to SD=0.13. Her LEI profile was very positive; on the satisfaction scale, she scored higher than any other teacher in the experimental group (see Figure 4.2, teacher 4). Observations revealed a steady shift from a teacher-dominated to a more student-centered style of teaching with frequent instances of group learning. The rapid evolution of her teaching style may indicate that school-based innovations are a good medium for the professional development of novice teachers.

Bat Sheva: The overall picture which emerged from Bat-Sheva's teaching performance was completely different. The average criterion standard scores in the comprehensive groups were about 2 SD higher than the corresponding classroom standard scores. Her LEI profile was rather 'flat' (see Figure 4.2, teacher 15). The observations showed that she was very dominant in the classroom and took most of the initiative. Even when she apparently allowed group (paired) learning, she constantly provided the right answers, thus preventing independent student learning. Her behavior appeared to be unreflective: In the new heterogeneous MA setting, she clung to her teacher-centered style. Addressing an imaginary class average, she *ignored* and, therefore, *neglected* the 'comprehensive' students. The fact that the classroom scores of these students were much lower than their corresponding criterion scores shows that their abilities were grossly underestimated by Bat-Sheva.

The individual findings of all the observed teachers were presented and analyzed in the final report in a way that preserved teacher anonymity. By combining the outcome of three instruments of evaluation, we were able to demonstrate the existence of two main types of teacher within the school: The first type is a reflective teacher who conceives her/his role as that of a developer of the learning abilities and motivations of each student, adhering to the assumption that 'anyone can learn' (in Osnat's words). The teachers of the second type see themselves mainly as transmitters of knowledge to an abstract average academic student: They may lead some academic classes to good results (although Bat-Sheva's LEI scores did not show that the academic students particularly appreciated the atmosphere in her class) but display little interest in the problems and difficulties of less able students. With such teachers, weaker students will tend to perform below their ability level (see higher criterion standard scores of Bat-Sheva's comprehensive students).

Discussion and Conclusion

Our basic argument was that even in autonomous schools, self-evaluation is best performed by means of a partnership between two unequal yet complementary parties: practitioners and external researchers. Such a partnership provides the framework for a reflective dialogue between the two.

The usual conventional intervention of external researchers or consultants in schools is mainly prescriptive: The researchers impose their own theories and their own perceptions of the situation, and teach the practitioners how to apply these in their schools and classes. Inspired by Schön's ideas that *practitioners do not learn by applying someone else's theories*, we tried to establish a reflective dialogue in the sense of enhancing the ability of our participant teachers to reflect on their actions and to better understand the link between their behavior and their assumptions or beliefs. Thus, we assumed that the teachers would conceptualize their actions and construct their own theories of teaching in MA settings (Schon 1983, Clandinin 1985, Elbaz 1981).

Our reflective dialogue started from a purely practitioner-initiated activity, namely, achievement tests that had been developed and administered by the teachers. The results, as analyzed by the practitioners, at first appeared to be discouraging. By involving the partici-pants in a careful analysis of their own findings, we were able to make them reframe their expectations and their conclusions; in other words, to realize that the findings had actually uncovered some positive trends. No harm had been done to the comprehensive students, academic standards had been maintained and, according to these standards, a tangible number of comprehensive students had performed as well as the average academic ones, or even better. So after all, the conclusion appeared to be that the MAT experiment *had been successful* in their school.

In an attempt to obtain deeper insight into the implications of the results, a new approach was adopted, which involved the evaluation of the outcomes of the experiment at the level of the individual teacher, because it was the individual teacher who carried out the actual implementation of the MAT. Thus, the question *"Did the school succeed in implementing the recommended strategies and behaviors of MAT?"* as a result of the examination results became, *"What were the strategies and behaviors of the teachers who succeeded best in MAT?"*

At this stage, the teachers' perceptions of the link between action, beliefs, and outcome had become more coherent. A similar process occurred in subsequent stages of the dialogue, when different instruments were used (LEI, classroom observation).

As a result of the dialogue, the school management became ready to accept, appreciate and use the conditional, non-absolute answer, which emerged from the combined findings of three instruments of evaluation, for further decision-making: *Certain specific teaching behaviors which create a certain learning environment increase the probability of implementation of MAT, with reasonable success.*

The ultimate aim of a reflective dialogue such as the one described here, is to improve the practitioners' ability to make second-order changes (Bateson 1968). This phase of the process of decision-making appears to be crucial. An innovation may often not lead to the expected changes simply because of the inability of the participants to interpret their findings in a new and useful way. This is why the type of 'dialogue' described here – which starts from the needs of the school staff, involves them in the implementation and the evaluation of their actions, and ends up with the staff being able to make its own decisions – may truly be considered a process of *self-evaluation*.

School Evaluation as a Dialogue

What have we learned about the dialogue, about the partnership between teachers and researchers, beyond the direct conclusions drawn from this case study? And what have we learned about our roles as evaluators within such frameworks of school evaluation? I shall begin with the first issue of the dialogue and try to elaborate how partnership was gradually developed:

1) Partnership as a dynamically evolving process

Our partnership began as an 'asymmetrical partnership' in the framework of a school-renewal or school-improvement project. The teachers were conceived as the most sensitive party in terms of identifying the school problems, and as main figures for dealing with and resolving them. Our role was to develop the teachers' awareness to their potential; in other words, facilitate a process of personal professional growth. I see this phase of the partnership as asymmetrical in the sense that teachers, although an important resource for problem resolution, are still fully dependent on the researchers.

The second phase of partnership began with the initiative of the new school principal to establish a 'management group'. The problem identified by the group was how to improve the school image in the eyes of its clients; how to make the school more attractive and meaningful for the students. The diagnosis reached, indicated that there was no social integration between the two populations of the comprehensive school, the academic oriented and vocational-technical oriented students. It was decided to mix them in mixed-ability classrooms and experiment unstreaming, or mixed ability teaching (MAT).

I see this partnership as a more symmetrical one: Although neither party changed their roles, by spelling out their goals, the teachers assumed a more leading role. They were ready to disclose covert undercurrents and to translate them into explicit problems that needed to be tackled. They were more able to face the discrepancy between their manifested ideology of 'equal opportunity' and the actual school reality, namely, their theories-in-use. My main role as facilitator in this second phase was to initiate a process of inquiry.

The third phase of our partnership (not reported here) was an action-research setting in which we jointly implemented the MAT experiential framework. The heads of History and

Scripture departments, acted as facilitators of the two experimental groups of teachers, while we, the researchers, facilitated the 'reflective group', which consisted of all of the participating teachers. Our role was to collect the classroom observation data and to negotiate the terms of observation with each teacher. I regard this phase as an *equal partnership between unequal professional partners*. The teachers are professionals in their subject areas and the researchers, in the area of reflection. As such, we were complementary.

The fourth phase, the phase reported above, was a direct continuation of the third. It started with the management's direct request to evaluate the project and our idea to use the evaluative report not only as a 'product' (a tool for decision-making) but as a means for self-evaluation. I believe that it is in this phase that our partnership finally began to function as a real dialogue.

Conceiving our role as triggers of organizational learning, we chose to involve the school, teachers as well as management, in a critical reflection of their actions (Argyris and Schon 1978). As a result of this process, they came to realize the complexity of the school as a system. Self-evaluation became an exercise for practicing multi-variable situations, and circular instead of linear thinking.

Yet, to reach this new understanding, we, the researchers, were just as dependent on our partners. As practitioners, they were the real actors; they had to change their ideas of teaching in MA classrooms. They had to understand the inter-connection between their behavior, their students' learning and achievement, and their classroom climate. A reflective dialogue between equal partners, which triggered the interplay between action and theory, led to mutual understanding. Neither party alone could have reached the decision necessary for achieving a second-order change.

Thus, we came to understand partnership as a continuous dynamically developing process, going through phases as it gradually reaches the stage of mutual trust and becomes a 'real dialogue'.

Our role as evaluators in such partnership settings

The stages of growing partnership, described above, can be seen as stages of growth or development of responsibility on the part of the school. This formed the basis of our choice to implement 'Democratic Evaluation.' The concept 'democratic evaluation' was introduced by MacDonald, who argued that:

> Once we accept the idea that evaluation of educational programs or policies belong to public domain, namely, that such an evaluation is to provide a credible source of information to a range of audiences, then evaluation needs to be conceived and conducted as an independent service for all those who have the right to know.
>
> (MacDonald et al. 1975)

This immediately raises the question as to *who* is this audience that has the right to know? Stake, for example, claimed that parents, teachers and taxpayers all have the right to judge the value of curriculum (Stake 1967). The same view was voiced by Parlett and Hamilton, who declared that the evaluator had to acknowledge the interests of all such groups and, therefore, he cannot provide a simple 'yes' or 'no' answer (Parlett and Hamilton 1972). They referred to evaluation as both 'illuminative' and 'responsive' with respect to the evaluator's role as responsive to constituent interests.

Recognizing the pluralistic nature of society and the evaluator's obligation to democratize his or her knowledge, democratic evaluation takes the most extreme position:

> The evaluator...has no right to use his position to promote his personal values... His job is to identify those who will have to make judgments and decisions... and lay before them those facts of the case that are recognized by them as relevant to their concerns.
>
> (MacDonald 1978)

This aspect of *value preference* coincides with Cronbach who emphasized that the task of evaluation was:

... not to help people decide between alternatives, but rather to contribute to the dialogue, and help shape understanding of social programs and policy... not to produce authoritative truths but to clarify, to document, to raise new questions... (Cronbach 1980)

Following this trend, of evaluation as a process that provides a credible source of information to a *range of audiences*, we saw the participating teachers (rather than management) as a first-order audience. Moreover, we understood *illuminative evaluation* in terms of the process, namely, illuminating the process of evaluation specifically for those who participate in it.

This formed the background to our decision to involve the participating teachers as partners in the process of evaluation. Intuitively, we wanted them to experience evaluation as a process of questioning, thinking and rethinking with respect to their own action within the project.

As democratic evaluators, we were in a delicate position, torn between our commitment to the school management and our obligation to democratize knowledge, and between our moral inclination (or duty) to protect the vulnerability of the individual evaluee. Elaborating on the issue of confidentiality, Helen Simons wrote: "The public's right to know must be balanced against the individual's right to be discreet" (Simons 1987).

There is no simple solution to this dilemma. For us it meant getting the participants' consent to every bit of published data. In other words, only selected extracts of classroom observation, endorsed by the teachers, were used in the report. To protect the vulnerability of the participating teachers, we were careful to guard our findings from the authorities by disguising all identifying details of the teachers and later, of the students.

In assuming a democratic stance to evaluation, we were able to establish a climate of mutual trust between evaluator and the evaluee; the evaluator had to be seen as supportive and not destructive in the eyes of the evaluated teacher.

This is why we see self-evaluation as a prerequisite for applying a democratic model of evaluation. If by competent teachers we mean teachers who are reflective not only in their private domain but also in the public domain, who are *accountable,* then it is our role to create the necessary supportive context.

EPILOGUE - the last phase of our partnership

As a result of our evaluative report, the school management decided to implement the MAT orientation throughout the 9th grade. This meant stopping student classification into three different tracks (academic, comprehensive and vocational), and dividing them instead into heterogeneous (MA) classrooms. The implication of such second-order change meant that the 9th grade would become a diagnostic year for teachers to become better acquainted with their students' scholastic abilities before they reach the upper grades. By extending the diagnostic period to the end of the junior high school, we assumed that the less able learners would have a better chance of catching-up.

This decision to stop streaming was to be implemented only in the following school year. Thus, the next year was to serve as preparatory year for parents to become acquainted with the new ideas, and for teachers to learn to teach in MA classes. However, for various reasons but mainly due to the change of principal, the decision was never implemented. Under the new circumstances, we decided to evaluate the impact left by the project, by tracing the 'school-memory.'

This job was given to Hadas, an ethnographer who had joined the research team. She made the staff room her field of study and visited it once a week, interviewing teachers, management, participants and non-participants of the project, as well as 10th grade students who had participated in the heterogeneous settings. Analysis of her 'thick descriptions' yielded a new report, which we presented to the new principal at the end of the following year. This report was not passed over to the staff. Instead, it was put away in a drawer and forgotten.

The report's findings had the capacity to illuminate the impact of the MAT project on the school. The heterogeneous (MA) classroom was viewed in the 'school-memory' as consisting of two groups ('academic' and 'comprehensive'), each retaining its own identity. These two divisive identities were clearly the result of one year of streaming. They had been non-existent in the elementary school attended by these same students. The collaborative experience of the two groups was seen as opening an opportunity to re-examine this framework, to disclose the more personal components, which may be common to the two groups beyond those that separated them.

The analysis of the data indicated that the meeting of the two groups in the heterogeneous setting, created a 'cross fertilization' between them, which proved beneficial to both parties. Thus, the B stream ('comprehensive') student was exposed to the learning orientation of the A stream ('academic'). They characterized this learning orientation simplistically: "As a result of learning, achievement is gained". Once this orientation was adopted by B stream students, they discovered they were able to learn and achieve, and by doing so, succeeded in breaking down the myth of the A stream.

The academic students' benefit stemmed from actually helping the comprehensive students to learn. At the same time, in order to maintain their advantage, they had to work harder. Thus, the achievements of the heterogeneous setting were twofold, improving on the scholastic as well as the social dimensions. These were seen as inseparable, as two aspects of the same phenomenon.

In terms of the teachers, it was shown that the heterogeneous setting created uncertainty, or ambiguity, by rendering the old learning materials inadequate. It meant having to revise them in order to adapt to each student as an individual. This change from a 'frontal' to a 'differential' teaching orientation, which required a search for alternative ways of teaching, led to the professional development of the teacher. Had the school continued on these lines, more teachers would have participated and, thereby, developed professionally.

On the school level, the analysis showed a gap between the teachers' and students' conception of the MA project. The students tended to see the school as an institution that opens up opportunities. The teachers (who participated in the project) did not perceive the school in this way. The researcher explains this gap as a result of the double message transmitted by the school authorities. One of her recommendations was to take this finding of poor communication seriously.

To sum up this ethnographic research, the two years experiment in the MAT project, which, in terms of the school size, covered only a small portion of the school population, seemed to have left a great impact on both the participating students and teachers.   This finding supports our assumptions concerning the potential of a partnership between researchers and teachers to achieve school innovation on a second-order level.

Appendix 1

The Eight LEI Scales Used in the Study

1. SPEED: the rate of progress of the class.
2. FRICTION: disagreement, tension and antagonism between teacher and students, or between students.
3. GOAL ORIENTATION: recognition and acceptance of goals by the class.
4. DEMOCRACY: democratic procedures in the activities of the class.
5. FAVORITISM: the tendency of the teacher to favour some students over the others.
6. SATISFACTION: whether or not students like the subject, the teacher and their classmates.
7. COMPETITIVENESS: The extent to which class members compete with each other.
8. DIFFICULTY: whether or not the students consider the subject-matter difficult.

Appendix 2

Observed Teaching Behaviors

1. Amount of '*teacher talk*' – i.e., total amount of time (in minutes) of the teacher speaking without eliciting student participation.
2. Types of *teachers' questions* (number of questions of each type):
   a) convergent (closed): teacher accepts only one answer
   b) divergent (open): different answers are accepted as legitimate;
   c) rephrased questions: teacher repeats the same question formulated in a different way.
3. Students' questions: questions *initiated* by the students (number).
4. Time devoted to *types of discussion*: (discussion is defined as a multi-directional student-student or student-teacher-student interaction);
   a) convergent (closed): led by teacher toward attaining one correct answer;
   b) divergent (open): various outcomes are possible;
5. Time devoted to *types of task* in which the students are actively involved:
   a) individual assignments (different students perform different tasks);
   b) group assignments: responsibility is divided between members of the group, cooperation or peer learning.
6. *Teacher's response to student-initiated* requests, initiatives, interventions (number):
   a) no response;
   b) teacher responds;
   c) teacher responds to non-verbal cues.
7. Type of *teacher's intervention during sessions of active learning (number):*
   a) teacher provides the right answer;
   b) teacher directs the students to the group;
   c) teacher directs the students to other sources of knowledge (books, etc.).

1) based on a joint paper: Keiny, S. and Dreyfus, A. "School evaluation as a dialogue between researchers and practitioners". *Studies in Educational Evaluation* 19 (1993): 281-295

Chapter 5

Collaboration as a Means of Creating a 'Community of Learners'

The idea of a 'community school' emerged following a phone call I received one bright day from a lady representative of a highly reputed private fund in Israel. When we met, she explained that their donation policy was to promote cultural and educational activity in the community. I never found out why she came to me, and it was the first time I had been approached personally to submit a proposal and state my financial terms. On my way home, I felt like a character in a fairy tale, who had been given the opportunity to make a wish and have the dream come true.

My metaphor for community school was a school that, rather than being fenced off from its surroundings, extended its boundaries to include its natural and socio-cultural environment. The emphasis is on the learning aspect of the community rather than it's social aspect. Accordingly, natural, industrial, and socio-cultural environments are regarded as *learning resources.* This view implies a new way of thinking about school, about subject matter, teaching strategies, and the learning process. It also entailed a change in our conception of the school-community relationship.

Already, while working on the proposal, I had a particular school in mind, Yerucham's comprehensive high school. Of all the school principals I had come to know, the young dynamic principal at Yerucham was sure to jump at my 'wild' ideas regarding change.

Yerucham is a small development town situated 25 miles from the capital city of the Negev, Beer-Sheva. Among its advantages is the unique landscape, which included a large natural crater and an artificial lake created by damming three small rivers, that changed the microecology in the midst of the arid desert environment. Yerucham is an industrial town, boasting a number of factories; for example, a ceramics plant and a bottle-making factory, both based on local natural earth resources, and a modern pharmacological and cosmetics industry. Demographically, its 6,000 inhabitants presented a mixed population of immigrants, most of whom in the 1950s came from Rumania, Morocco and India, as well as more recent immigrants from the Soviet Union.

Yerucham carries the stigma of failure. Indeed, much effort has been invested in its educational facilities in order to change this negative image and stop the outflow of bright students seeking better schooling elsewhere.

This forms the background to my story. A brief presentation of our conceptual framework of school change and the role we ascribe to teachers in this process, is required before continuing with our narrative.

School Change

The main aim of school innovation is usually to improve students learning. School projects, especially those that are Action-Research (AR) oriented, involve the teachers themselves in the process of change by having them take responsibility for developing their knowledge as a basis for action. The underlying assumption of AR projects is that the transfer of responsibility or ownership from top to bottom, that is, from the management level to the teacher level, entails a conceptual change, or a change in the teachers' role conception; a paradigmatic shift from the idea of teaching as applying theory, towards teaching as generating theory (Ebbutt and Elliott 1985, Elliott 1992, Stenhouse 1975). Teachers as theory generators are better equipped to cultivate their students as active and autonomous learners; students who take responsibility for their own learning as a knowledge construction process.

Thus, AR school projects can be viewed as sites for experimenting with new ideas, reflecting upon them, and reconstructing new theories of teaching (Schon 1983). These, in turn, bring about improved, more meaningful learning in the classroom.

The term 'conceptual change' has become a kind of umbrella-concept for different interpretations, stemming from different views of 'conceptions'. *Conception* has been used interchangeably with ideology, philosophy, personal knowledge, worldview, basic principles, belief, perspective, and subjective theory. All these terms convey the notion of '*a comprehensive organized body of knowledge*' held at a given point in time. According to our working definition, conception is not merely a cognitive term: It consists of schemes of concepts, which are developed as a result of actions and interactions with the world and, therefore, it is also anchored in a person's beliefs and basic assumptions. Finally, in a way not quite known to us, it influences action (Gorodetsky, Keiny and Hoz 1997).

Teachers' conceptions of their role form part of this general conceptual structure. Such conceptions reflect their beliefs or basic assumptions about the student (learning and teaching), about society and the goals of education, and about knowledge. Table 5.1 presents two alternative conceptions of the teacher's role: the instrumental and the developmental. In chapter 2 I showed that participation in AR school projects led to a shift from an instrumental to a developmental orien-tation. In this chapter, my aim is to show that this change of role con-ception reflects a higher-order change.

Using Batesons definitions (1972), I argue that second-order learning implies second-order change, that is, understanding the way a working system functions and restructuring previous knowledge. Third-order change involves *meta-learning* or learning about learning. Metalearning implies greater teacher awareness of the learning processes within the classroom. It means promoting student ownership and responsibility for higher-level learning. Moreover, by reflecting on their practice and scrutinizing the effect of their teaching, teachers shift their focus from merely observing relationships or feedback mechanisms among students within the classroom (or the school as an institution) *to include in their own observations, themselves as observers too.* Viewed cybernetically, this self-reflective enterprise forces them to recognize themselves as observers and accept responsibility for their observations, explanations and interpretations of the way they build their systems of knowing and acting epistemologically (Foerster 1992).

The Yerucham comprehensive school case study will be used to illustrate the process of teachers' higher order conceptual change.

The Comprehensive-Community-School (CCS) Project

The 'wild idea' of a Community-school, once presented to the Yerucham school principal, was accepted with enthusiasm by him and a team of leading teachers. My aim was to involve them in the construction of their own model of a Community-school rather than applying my model. Parents and other community representatives were invited to a general meeting.

The principal presented his vision of a commu-nity-school and called for those interested to join in the endeavor. The Comprehensive-Community-School (CCS) project thus established, consisted of groups of community people collaborating with teachers. Five different collaborative teams were formed: an Industrial-team; a Chemical-team; a Community-team, an Environmental-team, and a Scientific-team. Facilitated by graduate students, each team indulged in a process of School-Based-Curriculum-Development (SBCD) with the aim of constructing new curriculum units, linking the learning process to different institutions or other resources of the community.

Table 5.1: Two Conceptions of the Teacher's role

	Instrumental	**Developmental**
General orientation	"Technical Rationality"	Reflection in/on action
Epistemological aspect	Objectivism; knowledge is an external entity	Constructivism; knowledge is a subjective construction
Task Ownership	Teacher	Student
Assumption about the learner	Passive, has to be controlled; i.e., external motovation	Active, initiating; i.e., internal motovation
Teacher's responsibility	Instruct, transfer knowledge	Promote student's learning processes by providing opportunities for direct interaction with knowledge
Learning goals	Achievements as products of learning	Learning as a process

Five graduate students acted as team facilitators, supervised by me. They showed great sensitivity to the unique setting of the teams, adapting themselves to their diverse modes and pace of learning rather than clinging to a rigid model of teamwork. It soon became clear that this approach was justified in that it left space for participants to take initiatives and to contribute as partners.
Three different strategies of learning came into play:

(1) Learning through direct encounter of the participants with industries or institutions as workplaces.
(2) Learning from the students' experiences in these workplaces.

(3) Peer-learning through a 'dialectical process of reflection'
    within the teams (Keiny and Dreyfus 1989).

The proceedings of all team meetings were recorded,
transcribed, copied and distributed among the participants for
further reflection. They also became our database for
understanding the process of learning in the collaborative teams.

I shall start by focusing on the Industrial-team, which consisted
of teachers of Math, Technology, Sociology, Management and
Secretarial Studies, and of community representatives from two
of the industrial plants mentioned above. (see Figure 5.1) A
follow-up of the teams learning process will serve to provide
insight into the teachers process of conceptual change.

The Learning process in the Industrial Team

At the beginning of the project, the teacher participants of the
Industrial-team revealed an Instrumental-orientation in terms of
their implicit epistemologies and their assumptions about
teaching and learning. This is conveyed by their statements in the
early group meetings (presented in Table 5.2).

It is evident that they conceived the factory as a medium for
their students' practicum; a place to practice what they have
learned at school. We termed this conception of the relationship
between school and community the 'apprentice model'. For
example:

- Industry   is best suited for students of the mechanical
  stream...There they can learn how to be a mechanic, or a
  plumber...
- The factory provides the best opportunity to apply all that they
  have learned at school.

Some of the industry participants of the team actually
suggested, albeit not explicitly, an alternative model of the
school-community relationship – a 'system model'. While
careful not to give advice in curricular terms, they claimed that
the factory could serve as an example of a system, consisting of

many interacting sub-systems and maintaining an input-output relation with its environment.

Figure 5.1: **The comprehensive community-school plan**

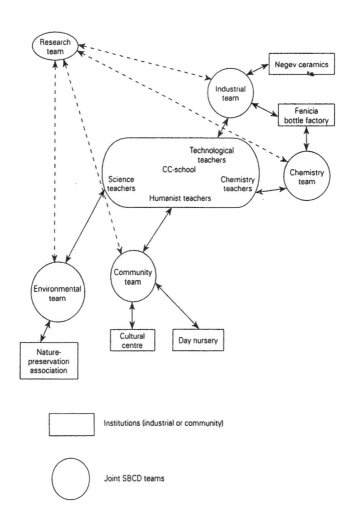

Table 5.2: Teachers' Statements Early in the Project,
Reflecting Their 'Instrumental' Role Perception

Epistemological aspect:

- My teaching is highly structured... That is how I manage to transmit a lot of material. I call this effective teaching.

- My main interest is to teach the formal curriculum so as to equip them with the knowledge required in the finals.

- I find myself explaining everything in great detail, so that they will understand.

Assumptions about learner:

- They are so passive and dependent, I could not give them any sort of independent assignment...

- Our task is to spoon-feed them...

- You have to make the connections for them. You cannot depend on their initiative.

Assumption about the teacher's responsibility:

- ...to transmit a lot of material in each period

- Where there is no control – there is no learning.

This idea of the factory as a system was vividly demonstrated by one of the industry representatives employed at the Negev Ceramics factory. Holding a ceramic tile in his hand, he explained:

> - When you look at the product, it is just a ceramic tile very simple... but just think how many processes are involved in its production: the basic materials; their transportation; weighing, grinding, and modeling; checking or quality-control at each stage; then wrapping, parceling, and storing, and finally marketing and shipping ...

The confrontation between the 'apprentice model' and the 'system model' became an important issue in the work of the team, guided by the facilitator.

The team was invited to visit the Negev Ceramics factory. The following excerpt is taken from the discussion that followed the visit:

Facilitator: - Allow me to suggest two opening questions: (a) What can we learn from a plant such as Negev Ceramics, a highly automated factory with very few workers? and (b) How can we use it as a learning medium?

Teacher: - I was struck by the scarcity of employed people. My prior image of a factory was of a row of workers along a production line.

Industry representative: - Today, every worker is a sophisticated worker. As for the second question, I do not see the plant as a learning place but rather as a trigger for learning. Visits (such as the one we have just expe-rienced) can best demonstrate this process to the students, triggering them to ask questions and later decide what they would like to investigate further. Learning should be carried out within the school. And, in any case, I wouldn't want to expose the kids too much to the conflicts among the workers...

Mechanics teacher: - I can see the advantage of exposing the students, especially from the lower streams, to the diversity and change of the factory. I would suggest that each student be attached to a specific worker, who would act as guide or mentor.

Industry representative: - This arrangement would provide very limited experience to the students, of rather limited skills, rather than broadening their horizon.

Facilitator: - I see here two different orientations: one, mainly advocated by the teachers, assumes that learning is achieved by following an expert and learning from him. The second, introduced by our community partners, focuses on the plant, the process, and the end-products, as a whole. The assumption here is that this would trigger curiosity and motivate the learner to follow his or her own inclinations, or specific interests, and engage in a personal-project type of learning. This second orientation naturally calls for a revolutionary change in the schools' vocational curriculum, whereas the first orientation requires smaller changes, which could be applied more easily.

Teacher: - I am for a compromise, a strategy that integrates the two approaches – exposing the students to the end-product or the factory first, and then each student could be guided by a specific worker.

Industry representative: - No worker has the time or the skills to teach kids and, judging from my experience, it takes a long time even for engineers in the plant to learn from practice.

Electricity teacher: - ...It is the repetition of activities that I find so important for mastering skills. The theoretical principles, I can teach in the classroom.

Community representative: - As I see it, there will be less blue-collar workers in the future; most tasks will be replaced by machines. Employees will have to acquire very different skills. They will have to be capable of technical thinking rather than technical skills.

Teacher: - What do you mean by 'technical thinking'?

Math teacher: - I think I know what is meant by technical thinking. I can give you an example from my perspective. To cope with the final exams today, my students require more than technical knowledge. They are expected to be able to tackle problems that they have never seen before. In other words, I have to teach them 'Mathematical thinking'... This discussion has given me an idea about how to introduce the subject of Statistics, which is a requirement for the Biology final examination. Instead of starting with a theoretical introduction, I could take the whole class to the factory. By watching how samples of bottles are taken out periodically for quality control, I could introduce them to 'statistical thiking' actualizing the basic principales by connecting them to concrete events.

This excerpt illustrates the teachers' discourse on learning from industry, or, in more general terms, on the relations between school and community. The ideas exchanged are not merely their 'espoused theories' but rather their 'theories-in-use' (Argyris and Schon 1978), which stem from their own teaching experience. The facilitators' main role in the process is to trigger the dialectical process of reflection in the group. By shifting the discussion from the concrete to the abstract level, and then dwelling on the tension between the two different models of school-community relationship, the facilitator promotes teachers' reflection.

Different modes of reflection are to be found in the literature (Carr and Kemmis 1986, Van Manen 1977, Handal and Lauvis 1987, Zeichner 1993). We see 'critical reflection', the highest level of reflection, as essential for the process of teachers' conceptual change. In our example, this is triggered by the facilitator by translating their familiar, routine way of teaching into a theoretical model or orientation and confronting it with an alternative learning orientation. The participants are then invited to examine the rationale of their model and the extent to which it fits their ideas of teaching. In other words, they are led to reflect critically upon their beliefs and basic assumptions.

Naturally, some teachers were slower to grasp the differences between the two models, and others (e.g., the Math teacher) were quicker to articulate them into general criteria, such as 'technical knowledge' versus 'technical thinking'.

Gradually, the team came to view the factory as a system, focusing their attention on the relationships between the subsystems, or different departments, as well as between the factory and its outside environment. This change of view is conveyed in the following excerpt taken from the Industrial-team meeting later in the year:

Teacher: - Before the project, I associated industry with technology only. Today, I realize how much more complex it all is. This small bottle-making factory, for instance, is a dynamic system. The different departments are its subsystems...

Teacher: - Students can analyze the product, what it is made of, how it is marketed, etc., and through this type of learning, they gain a wider outlook...This could help them in the future...facilitate adjustment to their future jobs, to their future milieu..

Teacher: - ...There is constant progress here...What today is considered a technological achievement, in a few years time will be practically obsolete, out of date.

These statements reflect a shift from a positivistic to a cybernetic orientation. Accordingly, a factory is seen as a system consisting of various interacting subsystems; a system adapted to changing conditions and to unforeseen problems. Yet, in von Foerster's terms, they indicate only 'first-order cybernetics'. In order to achieve 'second-order cybernetics', the teachers had to move from the first strategy, learning through their direct encounter with the industries, to a second strategy of *learning through their students' interactions* with the factory.

Curious to try out some of these ideas, some of the teachers organized class visits to the factories and other community institutions. The facilitator, encouraged this step, by making sure that student feedback was elicited, recorded, transcribed and fed back into the group.

The following excerpt is taken from the students' discussion following their experiences in a community institution:

- It all looked so simple when presented in the classroom, but in actual life there are so many different aspects... It's to do with relationships, with people's different frameworks...
- I am not merely dependent on the quota allotted for me by the boss, it is very much up to me, the way I meet their demands. I respond to people... It's sort of mutual. I sign my name, which for me is an indication that they trust my word.

Reflecting on this feedback, the teachers realized that their students were capable of taking more responsibility than the teachers had assumed initially. From their students' highly interactive and complex ideas of the working places, the teachers began to revise their prior assumptions about learning and plan different ways of teaching. This is reflected in the following excerpt taken from the Industrial-team meeting:

- We plan to open the curricular unit with a visit to the industrial plant. Only then, judging mainly by their reaction, by their level of involvement, will we be able to know where their interests lie.
- Let's not decide for them. Let them decide for themselves, otherwise we would be regressing back to our conventional framework, where teachers make decisions for the students on how to act.

In terms of their role conception, the participants of the Industrial-team had shifted from the Instrumental to the Developmental approach, as conveyed by their statements on the second year of the project (see Table 5.3).

One question remained open, To what extent did this change in role conception indicate a shift from first- to second-order cybernetics? In other words, To what extent did it imply a higher order conceptual change?

Conceptual Change - A Double-Locus Model

Let us go back to the interactive model cited in chapter 1 (Figure 1.1) According to this model, conceptual change is a process that occurs in two interdependent contexts, a social and a practical context. The social context is provided by the group in which the teachers exchange their different ideas of teaching and engage in critical reflection. This is analogous to our collaborative teamwork. The second context is provided by the teachers' actual practice, where they can experiment with their new ideas and reflect on or in action, namely their teaching experience (Schon   1983). In other words, they include themselves as observers and reconstruct their pedagogical knowledge. There is no necessary sequence between the two loci, the practical context can precede or follow the social context, but they are mutually dependent.

Table 5.3: **Teachers' Statements at the End of the Second Year Reflecting a More 'Developmental' Approach**

<u>**Epistemological aspect:**</u>

* Teachers cannot be the center of knowledge...

* Students can learn by a direct encounter with their environment, for example, their community or the factory...

<u>**Assumptions about learner:**</u>

* Students can observe, explain, evaluate, and judge things... Here they can actually learn by themselves.

* They discovered that they could use their initiative, that they can influence things... which gave them more confidence in their learning.

<u>**Assumptions about teacher's responsibility:**</u>

* This is an opportunity to do interesting things... to indulge in small group learning, where they learn by doing, through their own experience...

* Let's give the students the freedom to choose, to decide on their own course of learning.

We decided to shift our attention from the collaborative team, the social context, to the locus of practice, and follow up the teachers' implementation of their newly constructed curriculum units. In the following section, we focus on Batya, one of the participating teachers, who plunged into an experiential implementation of her new ideas in her own classroom.

Batya, a teacher of Home Economics, was a member of the Community-team. In her search for community collaborators, she formed a partnership with the staff of a well-equipped day nursery, with the aim of developing a curriculum unit entitled: "Child – Development". Her target population consisted of 14 girls, aged 16 to 17, comprising the lowest stream of the 11th grade, known for their lack of motivation and under-achievement. Her practical-context was formed by the staff of the nursery, including the regional coordinator and the pedagogical inspector.

In one of the Community-team meetings, she describes how she negotiated the terms of this partnership:

- It was important for me to lay down some basic rules, for instance, that the girls were there to learn and not as working aids... that I expected the staff to be patient and ready to answer their questions...

Practicing the New Curriculum

After many weeks of careful planning aided by her group facilitator, Hadas, a graduate student of Anthropology, Batya began to implement her newly developed curriculum-unit. She introduced the new curriculum by taking the whole class to visit the nursery. She directed her students in a very informal manner: " Look around. Direct your questions to the nursing staff Try to figure out the reasons..."

She allowed sufficient time for them to observe, wander about, pick up an infant or play with a toddler, etc. Once assembled (in a small open-plan room at the center of the nursery), she encouraged her students, again in an informal way, to voice their impressions: " What did you see? What would you like to know?"

Later she admitted her strong fear of her effort falling flat, her serious doubts as to whether their interest, their curiosity, would be aroused. Much to her relief, they had responded positively and by the end of the session, they managed to produce between them a list of some 10 different topics stemming from their own points of reference. For example:

* What happens if a child is hurt? Who is to blame? What is to be done?
* Why do babies cry?
* What are the requirements for becoming a nurse?
* Children's games in the playground.
* A lot of patience is needed for handling small kids.

(Note that the last two topics were not formulated as questions. Batya decided to stick to the original phrasing instead of trying to teach a correct way. In so doing, she felt she was legitimizing their ideas; enhancing their ownership).

Discussing the subject with Hadas, her facilitator, she voiced her thoughts:

> The shift of focus from Home Economics to child development formed the basis for my partnership with the nursery. Yet, only after we had started working on the curriculum, did I realize how vast was the range of subjects represented there. The girls actually had to cope with problems of education, diet, management, psychology...

Having succeeded in arousing their genuine interest, their desire to know more, she was now faced with the methodological aspect: How to proceed, How to tackle their questions, How to carry out the investigation.

This is where she switched to the reflective process in the Community-team, the social context of our model.   She presented her practical problem: How to proceed from their questions to the investigation. This soon developed into a topic of discussion and exchange of ideas. Together they constructed a new inductive method of learning whereby students would be guided to collect diverse types of data and, in this way, extend their knowledge on their specific topic.

Back in her classroom, Batya encouraged her students to collect information, each on her own chosen subject.   For example, on the question of why babies cry, to observe babies behavior; interview the staff; their own mothers, etc. As they gained confidence in the process of data collection, the girls' own initiative emerged, and they approached a local pediatrician for an appointment, as well as the school psychologist. Thus, more and more professional knowledge was accumulated.

Theoretical knowledge was carefully introduced by Batya, firstly, by using dictionaries. New terms, which the girls had collected, were looked up, for example, child–development, accident, patience, and many more. Secondly, a visit to the local library was organized, where more material was found for their different topics. This also became a major opportunity to expose them to books and to teach them how to use the library.

Relating her teaching experience in the Community-team, Batya says:

> ... Their files gradually filled up with field notes based on their own experience (experiential knowledge), observations (observational knowledge), and recorded interviews, etc. Spreading it all out on their desks, they realized what was missing: photographs to illustrate the childrens' gestures, behavior, body language, the general setting of the nursery. The very next day, they came with a pocket camera and took snapshots.

The general enthusiasm in the classroom spread, catching the more reluctant girls and, within a month, they were all working on their personal projects.

At this stage she handed out personal files, bearing the school logo. Apart from the practical aspect of storing all of the collected material, there was another dimension to the file; it signified transfer of responsibility with respect to knowledge, from the teacher to the students. It implied that the pool of knowledge was the learners' creation and, as such, the learner had assumed responsibility for examining, re-viewing, adding missing parts, to improve it.

There remained one last problem, which Batya chose to bring up at the Community-team meeting the 'social context' namely, how to end the investigation? How to formulate an answer to the original questions? This raised the whole issue of evaluation and, in particular - how to evaluate learning by inquiry? This issue was elaborated in the team at great length.

In her classroom, Batya chose to emphasize the diverse nature of the data collected and to confront, for example, theories about the welfare of babies with the nurses' or mothers' practical knowledge. To confront observational data versus reflective or interpretive explanations. Her implicit message was that there was no single, simple, correct answer.

The group discussions, on the other hand, led to the establishment of a framework for the written assignment. They decided to call the concluding chapter: "What I have learned or, how I evaluate my learning". Thus, the issue of evaluation was simultaneously dealt with in both loci: in the social context of the Community-team and in the practical context of the classroom.

The last excerpt, taken from the Community-team's discourse, conveys Batya's attempt to evaluate the process of learning in her classroom, a process that she had initiated and was responsible for:

> I cannot tell you how encouraged I am today by the progress in my classroom, especially in view of the fact that, initially, I had such low expectations from my under-achieving girls. Today, they are actually able to work independently, each on her personal project. Now I understand our main goal as enhancing the students' ability to become independent learners...

When asked to evaluate the project her respond is:

> There is the product (she points to the final assignment) and the process, that is, the learning process that led to this written work. But to me, the so called 'by-products' of the process are no less important. For instance, my girls actually learned to use the library. I see this as a most significant product... the implications of which are infinite...

Batya's experiential implementation of her new curriculum unit illuminates a number of important points, which can help us understand the process of conceptual change. First and foremost, in order to turn the nursery into a learning medium, she formed a partnership with the nursing staff. They were rather apprentice-oriented and inclined to see the girls as working aids rather than active learners. Batya learned to negotiate her terms and maneuver delicately between conflicting interests. Her intuitive idea of a curriculum unit that focused on child development had to be practiced and reflected upon before its potential could be revealed. She herself admits her surprise at discovering the wide range of subjects that unfolded from the topic. Naturally, this pilot experimental setting was accompanied by doubts as to the feasibility of such a curriculum and fears that it would not be found attractive by her 14 low-achieving girls. She knew only too well that they were capable of turning the whole endeavor into one big joke...

Some of these challenges she could handle alone. For example, negotiating norms of intervention with her nursery partners. Others had to be practiced first and reflected upon with Hadas, her facilitator. For example, after the initial visit to the nursery, in which the facilitator acted as an observer, they were able to carry out a reflective dialogue and deliberate at length on all of the details before finally eliciting the girls' personal topics from the discussion. Issues of a more general theoretical nature, such as inductive learning, or evaluation, she chose to thrash out within the reflective context of her peer-group. In this respect, Batya was displaying second-order learning. Aware of the different types of learning, in the different loci, she was able to make a decision as to when and where to use each. Meta-learning is reflected through her awareness of her students, her attempt to promote higher levels of learning, responsibility and ownership. Moreover, by taking responsibility for her own interpretation and explanations of the ways she builds her system of knowledge, she also acts as a second-order cybernetician.

Discussion

The optimal setting for teachers' conceptual change, is, in my view, the interactive double-locus framework, whereby conceptual change occurs in both the teachers' actual practice and a social context of the reflective team. School projects aimed at achieving conceptual change have to ensure a framework that provides the two necessary loci. Such a double setting was achieved in the Comprehensive-Community-School project. The collaborative teams, as sites for deliberation, for the exchange of ideas, and for the dialectical process of reflection in the group, served as a social locus. The classroom, as the site of experiential implementation of the new curricula units and participants' reflection on their actions, acted as a locus of practice.

To highlight the teachers' conceptual change, I chose to focus on the evolution of their idea of school-community relationship. The CCS project, by definition, was based on the cybernetic or system paradigm, whereby school is not seen merely as part of the community but maintains a dynamic interactive learning relationship with it. The project, although introduced from the outside, was presented as an abstract, open idea. Our aim was to trigger the participants to construct their own model of Community-school, according to their needs and within the constraints of the system. Thus, the success of the project depended on their mutual motivation and involvement. It turned out that the teachers reacted according to our expectation and used their initiative to invite community people to share in the process. Their community partners seemed to catch on, even though it required considerable motivation on their part to attend the team meetings after a long working day, and devote many hours of their free time to the project.

At the outset, the teachers were clearly anchored in the positivistic paradigm, adhering to the conventional idea of school as a place where theoretical knowledge is acquired (see Table 5.2). The participating teachers seemed unaware, initially, of the conceptual gap that existed between their conventional ideas and the orientation of the proposed project. Neither were they conscious of the radical epistemological change that it entailed with regard to their basic assumptions about learning and teaching, as well as on the school-community relationship.

The introduction of the system or cybernetic model by the community partners, and the confrontation between the two different models within the team, became the turning points in the process of the teachers' conceptual change. The interaction within the collaborative teams around the development of an integrative curriculum unit, helped them bridge the classical rift between theoretical and practical knowledge, whereby the school is regarded as a place for theoretical learning and the community's industrial plants or day nurseries, as sites for practice. Moreover, learning was finally understood by both teachers and students as a complex process of construction of subjective knowledge (Glasersfeld 1989). Accordingly, their idea of knowledge became multifaceted and multidimensional, conveying different representations of reality. Their encounter with the factories led also to their realization of the interrelations and interconnectedness of the different components of our reality and, thereby, to the impact of global changes (such as the European Common Market) on local factories, on community institutions (including schools), as well as on individual welfare.

Thus, teachers who, like Batya, actually implemented their curricular ideas became second-order cyberneticians with respect to taking responsibility for their newly generated knowledge. The "child development" curriculum clearly reflected Batya's observations, explanations, and interpretations of her way of building her system of knowing and acting. It stemmed from her basic egalitarian belief in the right of her low-stream girls to learn. In epistemological terms, it reflected her disposition toward the accessibility of knowledge. With respect to the school–community relationship, she saw it as her responsibility, her role as a teacher, to educate her students to become active responsible citizens, involved in their community's future welfare.

Self-Reflection or My Own Meta-Learning

Reflecting on action, in this case, on the CCS project, or the construction of a new model of school, was not merely a response to a challenge that had appeared out of the blue. I see it today more as actualization, growing from my deeply-rooted beliefs, which, at the time of action, may have been more implicit than explicit in my thinking. I have been exposed to cybernetics, to both Humberto Maturana and Ernest Glasersfeld personally, as well as to their writings, and had been fascinated by this alternative conception. My biological and ecological background may also have played a role in my scaffolding this newly developing educational paradigm.

Yet, to impose my ideas on my partners, the principal and the teachers of the school, would have been a wrong strategy, completely contrary to the idea itself. Instead, the Community-

School view was presented as an abstract, open idea, with the aim of triggering the participants to construct their own model of Community – school, from their own field of reference.

Here we were faced with the first dilemma. We could not expect the teachers to possess the same basic readiness. They were enthusiastic for various reasons; maybe, to some degree, *because* they had no idea how radical a change was required. Although both parties, researchers and practitioners, were using the same terms, and apparently talking the same language, conceptually, the practitioners were still captives of the positivistic paradigm.

The dilemma created when two groups of people use the same terms yet attribute very different meanings to them, was not new to us. We had confronted it in previous intervention projects (Gorodetsky et al. 1997). It was clear that we had to establish a common language before we could proceed with plans for change and improvement. Establishing a common language requires time and patience, commodities that rarely fit the usual 'process and effect' model of educational research. This may explain the failure of many bottom-up projects, which, due to lack of patience, revert back to the safer game and more conventional methodology.

The name of the game is 'conceptual change' in the sense of a paradigm shift from positivism to the cybernetic or system paradigm. This is where our model for conceptual change comes into play. I believe this CCS case study substantiates it.

Our focus in the CCS project was more on the teachers' development and change and less on their partners, the community people who, however, evidently underwent a parallel change. We, the researchers, achieved a second-order change in terms of meta-learning, of gaining a deeper understanding into the process of learning.

We realized the powerful impact of the model's social–locus, the reflective group as a *heterogeneous* context and the important role played by the different images, the different ways of looking of the partners. For example, by introducing the alternative 'system-model', the industry partners offered a new image of a factory. This led to exposure of the teachers' 'apprentice model', which, albeit implicitly, was responsible for the school's vocational orientation. By juxtaposing the two models, the facilitator was able to negotiate and reconstruct a new joint meaning for the concept.

Constructing joint meaning does not imply or necessarily lead to consensus. Participants can still hold different opinions and do not have to agree. However, they do arrive at a common understanding as a basis for further negotiation. In this sense, they succeed in bridging the primary language gap and become equal partners within a 'community–of–learners', the reflective social context of the model.

Another aspect highlighted by the CCS project, *was to extend the idea of school-environment relationship*. Out of the five groups, each consisting of teachers collaborating with community members, the Environmental-team seemed the most obvious. The Biology and Geography teachers were already well acquainted with the representatives of the Nature Preservation Society, their partners in the team. They all adhered to the idea of using the natural environment as an educational resource and began developing a new curricular unit. The first activity planned of the crater (only five miles away from the school) fell into the pit of a conventional classroom activity. Instead of enhancing the students' motivation to investigate the phenomenon, the teacher stood in front of the beautiful desert landscape and *interpreted* what they were seeing.

A similar fate befell the Scientific-team consisting of Chemistry teachers collaborating with scientists from the R&D unit of the Phoenicia bottle factory. The focus of their partnership was an up-to-date equipped laboratory, where the students were invited to develop their individual studies. Here, too, the leading teacher was caught by the potential of the sophisticated chemical equipment. Thus, instead of triggering the students to generate research questions from their field of reference, they reverted to the instrumental role conception of teachers being responsible for knowledge transmission.

What could be learned from the two examples of failure? In both cases, no real partnership was developed. This was not due to the factor of personal-relations, which was friendly in both teams. It seems as though a friendly climate often hinders the process by trying to maintain the good atmosphere and refrain from disturbing it. To establish a real partnership, the group has to recognize the diversity of its members and allow the time and space necessary for voicing and thrashing out their different perspectives.

In the Environmental-team, in particular, there was no attempt to question the teachers' strategy of teaching or reveal the gap between the group's manifest ideology or espoused theory and its behavior or theory-in-use. What is the role of the facilitator in such a situation? Should he/she have provoked the participants? Might his/her reluctance have been intentional? These questions are left open.

When using an action-research orientation, we are faced with many constraints. In our particular context, these are anchored in the particular teachers, the community partners, and the research students acting as facilitators. The fact that both the Industrial and Community teams succeeded and the Environmental-team did not, highlighted the possibilities that lie dormant in social-cultural and technological environments as learning resources.

Chapter 6

A Community of Learners: Promoting Teachers to Become Learners

The subject of this chapter is the collaborative group of teachers and researchers involved in the STES project. We met them first in Chapter 1, where they served as the context of practice to illustrate the learning process within a 'community of learners'. The teacher participants came from an environmental education (EE) high school, and the researchers from the two institutes of research in Sdeh-Boker, a campus of the Ben-Gurion University of the Negev: The Scientific Desert Research Institute (DRI) and the Ben-Gurion Archives (BGA) for Recent Jewish History Research, both are attempts to impliment Ben-Gurion's vision of the Negev desert as a challenge for generating novel ideas and creative solutions, in terms of science, technology, and society. A 'Unit for Environmental Education' (UEE) was added in the early eighties, whose task was to promote the Environmental Education (EE) orientation through curri-culum and teacher development.

The Environmentl Education high school, which was affiliated to the UEE is a boarding school whose target population consists of nature-loving students from all over the country. It has developed a unique EE core-curriculum, which is basically interdisciplinary, system-oriented, and aimed at integrating students with their environment. Heading the EEU, our first task was to conceptualize the EE core-curriculum to a theory of practice, termed "Sdeh-Boker Version of Environmental Education"and to construct a model for EE curriculum development (Keiny et al. 1982).

Various changes have taken place in the school since. The founding-teachers have mostly been replaced by new ones, less committed to the EE ideology. The school has succumbed to the demands of regular high school curricula, has lost much of its uniqueness and its attraction for the selective population of students that it enjoyed in the past.

This forms the background to my story about the STES collaborative educational endeavour. Collaboration has become a slogan in educational research. As noted by Hargreaves (1994), it is often a case of 'contrived collegiality' imposed from above and serving the management (whether of a school or of a higher rank) to perpetuate the existing order. Collaboration, in our case, is not an end but a means for creating a 'community of learners' consisting of teachers and researchers, all of whom are recognized as professionals, albeit of different kinds, indulging in a mutual process of learning. Learning is based on their joint experience, which they strive to conceptualize into a new theory of teaching/learning practice. In this respect, they are *partners in knowledge reconstruction*.

In terms of the learning process, our idea of a learning community is very different from the commonly used concept of learning according to which 'expert knowledge' is transmitted from researchers, who are seen as 'knowledge producers' to the teachers, who are seen as 'knowledge users.' We, the researchers, did not act as experts in this respect, and the teacher participants were also generators of professional knowledge. In Goodson's terms, learning involves a valuable 'trade-in' between two parties differently located in structural terms (Goodson 1992), producing true collaboration and the capacity to develop a new narrative of action, and empowering the teachers as a group to acquire a fuller picture of their work, and thus, fuller control of their professional lives.

True collaboration is voluntary, not imposed by an outsider. Participation in the project was likewise based on free choice. However, the reason for joining was not the same across the different parties. I shall discuss my reasons for initiating the project, and then elaborate on the other participants' motivations for joining the adventure.

STES - A National Trend

A call to integrate science, technology and society was made in 1992 by a national committee, whose task was to evaluate science education at all levels of schooling. The underlying rationale was that by treating science and technology as social phenomena connected to everyday life, these two subject areas would become more relevant and meaningful. In response, a proposal for an STES (Science, Technology, Environment and Society) project was submitted, and accepted. The project encompassed three universities collaborating with a number of schools. Our story is about our work in one such school, the EE high school in Sdeh-Boker.

The STES approach, although similar to EE, places emphasis on the societal context and the complex relationship between the different sectors of modern society. Science and technology, as important aspects of our society, are also closely connected with social as well as environmental problems. Thus, the explicit aim of the STES project was to develop curriculum units that would broaden awareness and create a sense of responsibility with regard to real social and environmental problems.

The STES project gave me the opportunity to revive the ideas manifested in the Sdeh-Boker version of EE and to formulate the implicit ecological conception (introduced in Chapter 1), more explicitly.

Creating the Group

As already indicated, in a true collaboration, each member joins voluntarily rather than being compelled to do so. When I introduced the STES project to the principal of the EE high school, he suggested I meet Hava, a leading teacher, whom he thought might be interested. Hava listened patiently to my brief sketch of the project (which was then not very clear even to me) and came up with an alternative idea, initiated by a team of three teachers: Hava, a Biology and Geography teacher, Dan, an English and Computer Science teacher, and Oren, a History teacher.   During the summer vacation, the team submitted a proposal for a new integrative curriculum for 10th graders entitled, "Desert and Desertification". The proposal's main focus was to involve the students in individual research studies on topics that they themselves chose, under the general title, "Desert and Desertification".

Another important aspect of the project was to use the Internet as a way to collect information from different countries. Announcing their curriculum as a Kidlink project, they invited Netters, teachers, students, and researchers, to join the adventure of learning about the desert and desertification.

By the time of our first meeting, the first responses from Alaska and Australia had already arrived. By the end of the year, some 50 teachers and their students, from all over the world, were Internetting with the school

Judging from the teachers' manifest objectives, which were enumerated in "Desert and Desertification: Notes for Teachers", their aims seemed congruent with those of the STES project. In terms of the teacher's role, there was a clear emphasis on the teachers' responsibility in formulating the content as well as the pedagogical basis of the curriculum.   The idea of a learning community as a site for a mutual process of learning between different parties (teachers and students), and where students could develop as autonomous learners, was similar to our conception of learning. I was particularly attracted to their idea of technological environment in the sense of opening new tracks of information,   or extending the concept of curricular knowledge.

The school principal, while endorsing the teachers' initiative, had his own ideas about school change, which he voiced somewhat later (in a joint meeting of high school principals initiated by the Education Department of my University). He believed that teachers should be given the opportunity to teach their pet subject or topic, apart from their regular formal obligations. Thus, a special niche would be allotted within the timetable for a wide range of topics as an open choice for the students. The basic assumptions underlying his rationale were:

(a) that teachers need this outlet to compensate for their burdensome obligations;
(b) that they teach best those topics that are of personal interest to them, and
(c) that an open supermarket of subjects gives the student the opportunity to choose and, thereby, to indulge in more meaningful learning.

Thus, he did not believe in radical changes. Times had changed and educational ideologies, like environmental education, had lost much of their old glamour. According to him, school change should be interpreted by each teacher in his or her own way. He saw his role as principal in terms of granting the space to act and to ensure the necessary means.

The teachers and the principal were keen to create a framework of collaboration with researchers from the two research Institutes. I believe that apart from gaining their assistance in supervising students' projects, they saw them as neighbors and parents, as part of the Sdeh-Boker community.

The idea of involving researchers in the collaborative framework was discussed with the directors of each of the Institutes. Both accepted the initiative and suggested that they would sound their people and pick the candidates for the project. Thus, six more participants volunteered: Saar, a desert architect, Moti and Ruth (who was also a parent of one of the participating students), desert agriculturalists from the Desert Research Institute; Avi and Edna, two graduate students of Jewish Recent History, and Orna, a curriculum developer, all three from the BG Archives Institute. Aviva, a Physics teacher joined the teaching staff. Altogether, we were four teachers, six researchers, and myself, as facilitator.

What were the researchers' motives for joining in? Evidently, each had his or her own reasons for joining. As we shall see later, they had no idea what was entailed. I believe they were all open to new ventures and sensitive, either as students, lecturers, or as parents, to the need to bring about change in the teaching and learning context.

As for my own fundamental interest in promoting change, I saw collaboration between teachers and researchers as a means of creating a 'community of learners', as a medium for mutual reflection and conceptualization of professional knowledge. In my mind, the STES project could serve as a site or framework for teachers' curriculum development, coupled with personal professional development. Moreover, as a model of collaboration between the academic world and the school, I felt that the STES project offered an opportunity for radical conceptual change. I shall elaborate on this point later.

The Framework of the STES Project

As can be seen from the above chain of events, the framework of the STES project was based on improvisation rather than pre-planning. It consisted of three different contexts:

(1) a reflective multidisciplinary group of four teachers, six researchers, and myself as facilitator, representing a wide and multidimensional conception of the desert and desertification (shown in Chapter 1);

(2) a 10th grade classroom which would serve as an experiential site for the teachers to practice the new curriculum, and

(3) the Internet, a site that connected the teachers and later their students from different countries, such as the USA, Japan, Peru, Canada, France, England, Alaska, Australia, and many others.

This framework was also consistent with our Double-locus model of conceptual change, elaborated in Chapter 5. In the model (see Figure 1.1) the teacher (T) is exposed to two interdependent contexts, one social and the other practical. The social context is our collaborative group of teachers and researchers and the practical context is the classroom, where the new ideas are tested and reflected upon; where teaching experiences are conceptualized and practical knowledge reconstructed.

Thus, the STES framework provided an optimal setting for the participants (teachers and researchers) conceptual change.

Conceptual Change

As mentioned above, the different interpretations of conceptual change stem from different views attached to the term conception. Conception is viewed by us as a mental structure that includes a person's beliefs and basic assumptions, some of which are tacit. It is a schema of concepts developed from theoretical studies, from practice and from interactions with the world and society. A conception is a dy-namic entity that can undergo changes based on practice and/or exposure to other sources of knowledge. Such changes can be enhanced by a process of reflection, which helps construct and re-construct professional knowledge (Gorodetsky et al. 1997). Accordingly, conceptual change does not pertain to cognitive mental perspectives concerned with change or evolution of specific concepts, such as mass, energy, heat, growth or health (see Driver, Posner, Vosiniadou, Duit and others); it pertains to experiential perspectives of conceptual change as proposed by phenomenographers (such as Marton, Linder and others) and implies a more radical, paradigmatic change, or *a change in a persons relationship with the world.* (Marton et al. 1997, Gorodetsky and Keiny 2002)

It is this notion of conceptual change that underpins the rationale of the STES movement in general, and our STES project, in particular. The significance of science knowledge for the actual life of the students is emphasized in STES. Accordingly, students are expected not only to understand the natural and technical phenomena around them, but also to become aware of the impact created on their lives by a society dominated by technologies of many kinds, and to take responsibility for dealing with existential authentic problems. In this respect, *context* is seen as an integral aspect of cognitive events.

Educationally, conceptual change implies a shift from the positivistic orientation underlying the way science education (as well as other subjects) is implemented in the school curriculum, towards a new curriculum based on the cybernetic or ecological paradigm. This entails a change of the teachers' epistemological views, more specifically in their view of what scientific knowledge is and what is the nature of science iself, as well as a change in their meta-cognition, or their view of the learning process.

Analysis of the Group Discourse

In the following, I shall relate the story of the group. The proceedings of its weekly meetings were audio-taped, transcribed and distributed among all participants to be used as a basis for further reflection. For me, they served as a database, which I studied over and over again in my attempt to arrive at an understanding of the learning process of the group.

This database, which I called the group-discourse, or group-narrative, I see as an independent entity, a group-self (Avraham 1972) without di fferentiating between what was said by whom. I was looking for a method of analysis that would best preserve the dynamics of the discourse, as well as its interrelation with the action it initiated and reflected upon. My first step was to identify and extract the major themes emerging from the 29-meeting discourse:

The First Theme: The Desert

The desert, as the key topic of the curriculum unit that we were aiming to develop, was naturally one of the first central topics in our discussions. The following excerpt, taken from the first group meeting (2.10.1994), illustrates the exchange of ideas on the role of the desert in the curriculum:

Dan: - I would like to emphasize that our choice of the desert stems from our world-view.
Oren: - My goal, actually the reason for my joining the project, is to find a way to make learning a more attractive and interesting

activity. The desert as an interdisciplinary topic has the potential to open up, to motivate, the kids.

Orna (researcher): - I would appreciate it more if we opened the concept to include the spiritual aspects ... not merely the desert as a physical entity. For example, the idea of man coping with the desert.

The desert was the central issue of the curriculum yet in the above excerpt it is clear that "desert" is conceived differentially by the participants. Some saw it as value-laden (a world view), others as an interdisciplinary topic which could trigger the students' motivation to learn. As a humanistic researcher, Orna was concerned with the teachers' restricted, ecologically-oriented concept of the desert.

The idea of extending the concept was also picked up in the second group meeting (9.10.1994). Reporting on the teachers' working team, Hava says:

Hava: - We discussed how to connect the Internet to the classroom activities. A vivid description of the Peru desert, which lies along the seashore, came through the Internet...We thought of sending them a description of yesterday's flood in the Negev desert...

Orna: - Why not use this example from Peru to illustrate a different type of desert, thus extending the concept...

Dan: - The idea is to see it as another source of information.

The three teachers in this short excerpt each regard the Internet as a main issue in that it enables the collection of different descriptions of the desert, from different national, regional, spiritual and personal perspectives. The researchers emphasis is on the desert as a concept and how the Internet could help in developing it. At this early stage, the main role of the Internet was seen in terms of extending the participants scope of information rather than as elaborating and broadening of concepts.

The desert as a multi-disciplinary multifaceted concept became the center of discussion in the 3rd group meeting (16.10.94).

Hava: - When asked what would they be interested to research, the students' answer was: the impact of the desert on man's way of thinking. Here is evidence that we are not stuck with the physical aspect only.

Avi (researcher from the BG Archives Institute): - I still don't see how I could be of help to the students. No one seemed interested in issues such as the desert as a strategic space for the State of Israel or Ben-Gurion (BG) conception of the desert ...

Moti (researcher from the Desert Research Institute (DRI): - ...or the Negev as an integral part of Israel's future...

Saar (desert architect): - ... or another example, what brings man to live in the desert? ...Or the desert as perceived by modern man. Such questions could well fit BG's vision.

This excerpt illustrates the researchers' growing concern that the concept of the desert should be broadened to include authentic current social questions. It was here that I sensed an underlying tension between the teachers' and researchers' idea of the desert. The orientation of the latter was closer to BG's ideology of the desert as Israel's largest potential area for cultivation and inhabitation. The teachers' orientation was more pedagogical, with the desert seen as a trigger for research questions, for students to define their personal project.

I suspected that this gap between researchers and teachers had deeper ideological roots. These were disclosed much later in the discourse, in conjunction with the issue of desertification.

Before moving to the next theme, I would like to emphasize the advantage of our method of analysis. By following one theme, in this case the desert, different aspects of our work were illuminated:

* Different meanings were attached to the concept by the different participants.
* The desert as a topic was shown to be of interest across the world, as a common denominator for creating dialogic connections through the Internet.
* The Internet and its pedagogical role in the curriculum was shown as a means to broaden our scope of knowledge, or to enhance deeper learning, or even to trigger the multidisciplinary, multifaceted aspects of learning.

* It disclosed the participants' more deeply buried ideological traps or the conceptual gap between the researchers and the teachers.

The Second Theme: The Participants' Conception of Their Roles

Another theme, which will be traced in the discourse of the first four group meetings, was the role of the researchers in the collaborative group.

In the first group meeting (2.10.94): I outlined my idea of group work and of the participants' role:

Shosh: - Our first objective is to build a collaborative framework based on an equal relationship between different parties, each professional in its own area. Our intention is not to help teachers, or teach them how to teach. The common goal of this group is to develop a new kind of curriculum, that is, a new way of teaching and learning.

After sketching what I meant by a new kind of curriculum, I continued:

The group's role is to form a reflective framework where we can question, inquire, plan, and test new teaching/learning activities, and thus, jointly construct our new theories of curriculum, of knowledge, of learning and teaching.

Although my words met with a general consent, I doubted whether I had actually succeeded in conveying my meaning. The two following responses illustrate this:

Oren: - I understood that the main role of this forum was to help us. Sitting around the table are experts in different fields. The students could be linked to these various fields, through you.

Saar: - Sure. We are willing to help the kids within the general framework, but my main interest, the reason I came here, is to develop a new methodology of learning.

Two different conceptions are revealed here with regard to the researchers' role. The teacher, at this early stage of the group work, tends to see the researcher as an expert, whose task it is to interest the student in his or her field of research. The researcher, on the other hand, sees his role in terms of developing a new type of curriculum.

Ruth: - We are aware of your obligations, your responsibility to teach, whereas I see our goal as a kind of watch-dog...
Avi: - As teachers, you are concerned with what to do in the classroom tomorrow, whereas we can philosophize, throw out ideas. You strive to be open to new ideas, yet you cannot free yourselves from thinking in terms of implementation.

This excerpt expresses the sense of disjunction between the parties. These differences were seen at this stage of the group work as obstacles or constraints rather than as a valuable asset. One way to overcome them was for the researchers to take part in and share the teaching obligations of the teachers. This was suggested later, during the same meeting:

Saar: - Would you mind if I attended your next classroom activity? I will sit quietly...
Hava: - Your presence could only contribute. Moreover, I would ask you to take part in the discussion, you could respond to the students' proposals.

Nevertheless, there was a lingering feeling of dissatisfaction on the part of the researchers. The visit to their Research Institutes only strengthened this sense of being used as experts rather than being real partners. This feeling was explicitly expressed in the fourth group meeting (24.10.94):

Saar: - I would like to see myself more involved and contributing....
Orna: -Are we a team of partners at all? It seems to me that you see us rather in terms of service-givers...

This theme of the participants' conception of their role could be rephrased as trying to understand the nature of the group collaboration. In my opening words, I defined collaboration as an equal relationship between different parties, each professional in a specific area. Yet it seemed these buzz words had not really made enough sense, in order to be directly applied in practice. By emphasizing that the researchers' role was not to teach teachers how to teach, nothing was said about what actually was their role.

It was only natural, therefore, that they were treated as research aids, as experts, whose task was to interest the students in their field of research, leaving them to feel used rather than being seen as true partners.

This issue will be pursued further in the following section.

Analyzing the Discourse in Terms of AR Learning Cycle

Cycles of Learning

At this point, I decided to change the methodology to the action-research framework of analysis. I did this because I realized that teachers development (and my own) to be an ongoing process of inquiry into one's own teaching of understanding of it, both on the micro-level of one's own context, as well as on the macro-level of the profession. Within the framework of the STES project, we were exposed to two simultaneous contexts of reflection, the practical classroom context, where the newly formed ideas could be tried out and reflected upon, and the collaborative reflective group. My role as a facilitator was to enhance reflection by modeling it, and to ensure a non-judgmental learning environment, where members would feel free to express themselves. Later, as will be seen, participants acquired the art of reflection and took over this role. However, all of us (teachers and researchers) were *learners*, learning through inquiry and researching our own actions. Accordingly, the group process could be analyzed in terms of AR learning cycles, each consisting the following four stages:

* Sensing a source of discomfort, or problem.
* Planning active experimentation.

* Experimenting and data collection, triangulation, etc.
* Reflection leading to new understanding, or to reconstructing pre-vious knowledge, to a redefinition of the problem (which leads to the next AR cycle)

Starting with the fifth group meeting, five cycles of learning were identified. Their analysis will illustrate the group learning process in terms of the themes identified above.

The First Cycle

1) Sensing or identifying a problem (5th group meeting; 4.11.1994)

Opening the meeting with a short reflection on the previous group meetings, I highlighted themes that had been raised, such as:

* The goals of our curriculum and how to reach them.
* The issue of interdisciplinarity.
* The different roles of the teachers and researchers.

I suggested that the group should decide on how to proceed. After a lengthy discussion, in which a whole range of new ideas was aired, the choice was made and the group decided to tackle a simple practical problem introduced by one of the researchers:

Ruth: - I would like us to plan the next classroom activity.

It seemed to me, at first sight, that the practical suggestion to prepare the next classroom activity was simply the easiest way out. However, later, during the planning stage, I realized there was more to it. Planning the next activity actually raised many issues, such as the role of the researchers, and interdisciplinarity.

2) The planning stage (continues in the 5th group meeting)

The researchers' motivation to be more involved coincided with the difficulties perceived by the teachers as to how to explain to the students their new way of teaching. This led the group to plan a joint meeting of the parties. The students were divided in small groups and, accompanied by a teacher, they met with a scientific researcher. The idea was to expose the students to interdisciplinary problems, as well as to the research activity of the Institute for Desert Research.

3) Data collection (6th group meeting; 11.11.1994)

The meeting opened with the participants' feedback on their meetings with the students:

Moti: - A group of 3-4 boys took part in the discussion; the others were passive.

Saar: - I tried to get them to talk but with a minimal success, only managing to squeeze out a few remarks here and there...

Orna: - I found them incapable of functioning on the abstract level. However, I believe that we were much more successful on the scientific-methodology level.

Dan: - We had no such problems in my group. The students were active and inquisitive, coming up with good questions.

4) Conceptualization (continues in the 6th group meeting)

Elaborating on the above findings, the group was able to disclose some of the deeper hidden, more tacit issues, such as:

* The students lack of interest in the project.
* Their feeling of uncertainty regarding what was required of them.
* Ambiguity is contagious and we seemed to have passed it on to the students.

The discussion, which was continued in the following (seventh) group meeting, closed the first cycle. In my summary, I reflected on the experience, describing it as an unfreezing stage, a reshuffling of some of our basic assumptions (such as the assumption about the researchers' ability to get the students' interested in their research, or the students' ability to see the relevancy of this research activity to their own learning). I suggested to them that 'unfreezing' was an important, even necessary stage for promoting higher-order learning.

The Second Cycle

1) Sensing, or reformulating the problem (7th group meeting; 18.11.1995)

The new question, which emerged from the first cycle of learning, was, How to trigger students' interest in this new type of classroom activity. (This was another way of questioning our function as a group.) After elaborating on the problem, it was then processed into a number of operational questions:

- How do we encourage students to generate questions?
- How do we open up more areas of interest?
- How do we create a framework that gives the students freedom of choice?

2) Planning (7th group meeting)

In the following discussion, different ways of teaching were suggested, portraying a whole range of educational and teaching styles. The decision of the group was to encourage diversity, let each teacher take his or her preferred course of action.

3) Data collection (8th group meeting; 25.11.1995)

The meeting opened with each teacher relating his or her experience in the classroom:

Oren: - I took them to the library, exposing them to seven files containing information on the issue of the desert, which I assumed would trigger their interest and generate questions. I admit, that I had only very moderate success.

Hava: - I wrote on the blackboard "Desert and Desertification", asking them to generate associations. It was very exciting.

Edna a researcher in the BG Archive Institute, reported the visit she had organized for Dan's students. The idea was to expose them to various sources of information and different ways of data collection (for example, personal diaries and authentic documents; computerized documents, original texts, Internet information, etc.). The students were then encouraged to try ways of retrieving information themselves.

Edna: - They became so involved that they were in no hurry to leave. They just stayed on and continued working. I admit that after all this talk about their indifference, their interest and personal involvement surprised me.

4) Conceptualization (9th group meeting; 30.11.1994)

The implicit message of the group was to legitimate the teachers to follow their personal inclinations and, by so doing, to enrich the group with a variety of examples. Thus, three different strategies of teaching were experimented. New goals were achieved by the collaborative strategy of a teacher and a young researcher, such as exposure of the students to a modern conception of an archive, where all documents are computerized. What was *not voiced* in the discussion were the more implicit effects of the visit, on both the teachers and students, regarding the biased attitudes towards the Ben-Gurion Archives. An undercurrent of tension emerged (which I had sensed already in the early group meetings) between Ben-Gurion's ideas of developing and populating the desert, and between the dominant 'green orientation' of the EE school, which emphasized preservation of the desert. Here the clash between the two contradicting ideologies was subtly disclosed, raising the teachers' awareness to these hidden assumptions, which they had not questioned before.

The Third Cycle

1) Sensing, or reformulating the problem (10th group meeting; 7.12.94)

It now seemed that the researchers from the Humanities had gained more confidence and were more able to voice their concerns. They claimed that as of now, the idea of desert and desertification had been dealt with in the scientific context only. Talking about the extension of knowledge, they felt that the more humanistic, historic and cultural aspects of the desert should be introduced. In this way, they argued, we would also extend the students range of choice, before they decided on their individual topics of study.

Their implicit question was: How do we extend the concept of the desert and, thereby, the range of potential topics for the students' individual studies?

2) The planning stage (12th group meeting; 25.12.1994)

This question was never brought up in the group. The teachers took the initiative and planned the new activity, reporting on it at the beginning of the meeting:

- Tomorrow we are going to expose the students to a totally different experience; a meeting with a desert landscape sculptor, at the break of dawn.

3)Data collection (13th meeting; 1.1.1995)

The teachers fresh experiences of their classroom activity in the desert were reported enthusiastically in the group:

Hava: - It was for me a most impactful emotional experience; the combination of his artistic ideas with the break of dawn over the Zin valley, was most powerful.
Oren: - The students were all there with him, responding naturally to his instructions, all behaved perfectly, no discipline problems... They said that they were immensely moved, though not necessarily agreeing with his views.

Aviva: - The sculptor exemplified a person capable of opening up new ways of looking. In this respect it was unlike any other learning exercise.

4)Conceptualization (continued in the 13th group meeting)

Reflecting on the data, the participant researchers began questioning the teachers on the nature of what they described as a moving experience. Why should this be considered a *learning experience*?

Moti: - We have to find out what was there that made the experience so special.

Orna: - Holistic learning maybe, which adds the affective and emotional aspects to the cognitive domain.

Saar: - Could we conclude that experiential learning is more effective?

Dan: - We repeatedly declare that the products of this new learning (about desert and desertification) will be different, and unique for each learner. This experience proved the case. Each of us teachers actually had his or her personal unique experience.

The scientists were still doubtful:

Moti: - I see here a breaking-down of the conventional learning framework. Is that what we meant when we started? I certainly had no such idea.

Two important points emerge in this cycle: Firstly, the group started functioning as a 'community of learners' in the sense of listening to each other and accepting differences. The humanistic researchers were able to make their point, which was taken seriously by the teachers, and turned into a classroom activity. The second point concerns the evaluative role of the researchers. As the teachers became carried away by the moving experience, the researchers took on the role of evaluators. By questioning whether the exposure to the desert landscape at the break of dawn could be regarded as learning, the discussion moved on to deal with higher-level issues such as what is considered as learning? This is what I mean by meta-learning.

The Fourth Cycle

1) Identifying a problem (14th group meeting; 8.1.1995)

How do we evaluate this type of learning?

2) Planning

Neither the identification of the problem nor the planning was done by the whole group. Taking the lead, the teachers planned their next classroom activity, and implemented it.

3) Data collection (14th meeting)

The meeting opened with the teachers' reporting on their activity:

Oren: - We took the students to a nearby spot, facing the Zin valley, gave them three sheets of paper, pencils, and ample time to record down their impressions in whichever way they wished. They sat there for over an hour in complete awesome silence, writing or drawing (displays the students' sheets). We did not interfere; we also sat down to work.

Hava: - For years I have been meaning to write something about the desert and never got around to it. Here it just poured out...

4) Conceptualization (continued in the 14th group meeting)

The teachers report opened a heated discussion in the group. The following excerpt illustrates it:

Oren: - The results indicate their sense of being at one with the idea of the desert.

Saar: - I cannot see any connection between these sheets of paper and our effort to trigger their inquiry, their observation. To what extent can we see this as a learning experience?

Dan: - I can see three points illustrating their process of learning: There is data collection, interdisciplinarity, and holism... I also see here   (in the sheets of paper), a junction between theoretical knowledge and other kinds of knowledge. To me the most

authentic knowledge is that of the learner himself, whether teacher
or student.

Shosh: - We have a new issue of discussion here: What is learning?

This cycle demonstrates clearly how the reflective group
brought the participants (mainly the teachers) to conceptualize
their experience of evaluating their students' learning. As typical
action-oriented teachers, they chose to cope with the question of
how to evaluate this kind of learning in the group, by action.
Instead of discussing the problem, they planned an activity but,
being good teachers, they also responded to this activity as
learners... By reflecting on their experience (as teachers and
learners), they actually raised the focal question, *What is
learning?* and tried to cope with it in an authentic and
meaningful way (see Dan's comments in the last excerpt). Had
they been dealing with the question within a theoretical context,
they would have probably cited their 'espoused theories' based
on Bruner, Piaget, etc., theories, which, as such, are not really
functional.

My point here is not concerned with whether their answers are
adequate, good or bad. I believe they point to a degree of
confusion and ambiguity (and, anyhow, who can really provide a
simple answer to the question, What is learning?). What I want
to stress is their attempt to deal with this higher-order question
*from their own reference point, from their own personal
experience.* This is what I mean by conceptualizing practice or
experience, and it relates to Dewey's idea of doubt as the
beginning of knowledge. Dewey believed that inquiry begins
with doubt, or from a confusing and obscure situation, and goes
on to make the situation determinate. The inquirer is not an
outside spectator; he or she is actually in transaction with it.
Inquiry does not remove doubt by recourse to a prior adaptive
integration, but by instituting new environing conditions that
occasion new problems so that there is no such thing as a final
settlement (Schon 1990, Prawat 1995).

The Fifth Cycle

1) Identifying or reformulating the problem: (15th group meeting; 22.1.1995)

What is learning, and how do we evaluate it? This question, first presented as a challenge by the facilitator at the end of the previous meeting, was taken up by the group:

2) Planning (continued in the 15th meeting; 22.1.1995)

Hava, the leading teacher, opened the meeting by suggesting that in the following week, due to the teachers' absence (for some reason or other), the group should lead the next classroom activity.

Hava: - ...not merely as baby-sitters. Feel free to plan the activity.

The next (16th) group meeting (29.1.95), attended by the researchers only, was dedicated to the planning of an evaluative framework, in which the researchers would interview the students. In order to learn about the progress made in their research projects, an open interview sheet was produced, which aimed to convey (first and foremost) their interest in the students' work and their desire to help. Its second purpose was to trace the progress in their individual studies, in terms of identifying a research question, choosing their method of data collection, developing original thinking, etc. Thirdly, by focusing on the students' understanding of key concepts, such as interdisciplinarity and desertification, the interview would try to disclose the students' conception of the new paradigm of learning.

After being endorsed by the teachers, this interview sheet was used simultaneously by four different researchers, each meeting with a group of 8-10 students. Judging by the students' feedback (which they related to their teachers) and by the enthusiastic feedback conveyed by the researchers, it could be said that the activity had been most successful.

3) Data collection (17th group meeting; 11.2.1995)

The meeting was opened by the researchers, who presented their respective interview findings (which in many cases was put in writing and copies were handed around). Gradually, as they related the details of their experience, a multidimensional picture unfolded, disclosing the students' conceptions of their learning and of their progress in both the classroom and individual studies.

4) Triangulating the data and conceptualization (continued in the 17th group meeting)

Triangulating the students' conceived learning with that of the teachers (as reported in the previous meetings) and the researchers, disclosed serious incongruities. These in turn led to critical reflection in the group, and to new understanding of the situation. It turned out that:

a) The students did not see the connection between their Desert and Desertification classroom activities and their personal research projects.
b) They felt that a lot of time was wasted due to lack of supervision.
c) The focus of the project for the students was the desert; desertification seemed irrelevant to them.
d) 'Involvement' being one of the declared aims of the project, they asked to be more involved.
e) They were totally unaware of our group's existence and our regular weekly meetings.

These points came as a shock to the teachers. Their reaction was a thunderous silence, while exchanging notes. It seemed that they were too hurt to be able to treat this information as a basis for reflection.

5) **Further conceptualization** (18th meeting; 18.2.1995)

I opened the meeting by acquainting the group with Kurt Lewin's AR cycle. Using the four stages of the cycle as criteria, I analyzed the last group meetings:

- Sensing or identifying a problem: how to evaluate the project?
- Planning an active experimentation: constructing an open interview ins-trument, as part of an evaluative framework.
- Data collection: collecting the students' feedback and thereby tracing their progress within the learning process; triangulating this data with the teachers' and researchers' feedback.
- Reflection that leads to new understanding; or reconstruction of our previous knowledge in terms of the students' learning process.

I stressed that this cyclic process (which actually stemmed from the teachers' request), was aimed at collecting data. The purpose of this data collection (some of which was sensitive and loaded) was to triangulate the students' feedback with that of the teachers and the group, and to highlight the incongruities and the multi-perspectives of the classroom activities. The aim of the process was to reach a better understanding about learning. Another way of looking at the process is in terms of the effectiveness of the group as a learning group; as a test of the degree of collaboration. I believed that our efforts to reach a better understanding of the issue (which was our stated aim) would also strengthen the group as a 'community of learners'.

Whether it was the impact of these words, or rather the time factor (a whole week to reflect on the new unexpected information), this opening triggered a flow of teachers' reactions:

Dan: - We have to go to the students and listen to what they have to say. They feel they are not being treated as partners. We should try together to build a collaborative framework.

Aviva: - They are at a stage in their research projects where they need more personal supervision.

Oren: - I believe we have to negotiate with the researchers as to who is responsible for what...

Edna: - We want to take more responsibility. I assume that by being more responsible, taking a more active part in the classroom, we will be less of a threat...

A reflective discussion followed, which led to some practical decisions in the group with respect to a plan of change. It was decided that we would invite students to participate in the group meetings, leaving them to choose their representatives.

The issue of desertification, which obviously had been neglected, would be the focus of the following classroom activity. Moti, one of the scientific researchers, was invited to give a talk on the subject and thus trigger a classroom discussion.

To conclude, the analysis of the group learning process in terms of action research cycles, serves to illuminate the gradual building up of the group as a 'community of learners'. The first cycle, which opened with the question, "How to involve the researchers in the classroom?" actually dealt with the issue of collaboration in the group. It ended with poor results, portraying little in the way of collaboration on the part of the teachers, who were not yet ready to accept the researchers as partners, but saw them rather as service-givers. The researchers, on the other hand, realized in this first cycle that succesful teaching is not a simple straight forword activity. Their assumptions about triggering the students' motivation by exposing them to their research projects, proved wrong. In the second cycle, another question emerged: "How to stimulate the students' interest and motivation?" Different strategies were tried by the teachers and the first vestigial signs of partnership emerged.

The third and fourth cycles became a turning point with respect to collaboration. The teachers took the lead in planning and implementing, and the researchers encouraged reflection and conceptualization. This new type of collaboration was based on different people playing different roles, yet maintaining an equal relationship by respecting each other as professionals. The teachers did not resent the researchers' role as evaluators, or their critical reflection, and were able to take on the challenge; namely, ask themselves, "What is the meaning of learning?"

This idyllic image of collaboration was somewhat disrupted in the fifth cycle. It seemed that the teachers, while encouraging the researchers to help in evaluating the students, were not yet prepared for collaboration in the sense of allowing their community partners to express themselves freely as persons. The feedback of their students was painful, and it took time for them to recover and be able to reflect on the situation from an outside perspective.

As the group facilitator, I had to cope with difficult questions, such as, How to create *a balance between learning as a growth process, and critical reflection.* How to allow participants to express their indivi-duality and, at the same time, remain open to the views of others. It seems that the teachers, by asking the researchers to take on the role of evaluators, unintentionally created an asymmetrical situation. Not wanting to assume the role of leader, I refrained from intervening, hoping to enhance, instead, the self-organizing nature of the group. Judging by the results, I am inclined to explain those painful moments as examples of learning, in which participants were forced to reflect on their action from a different point of view, and become liberated from their tunnel-vision. This was a time for self-reflective questions. In this respect, this last cycle witnessed a breakthrough in the group collaboration, after which they were better able to recognize each other's right to express themselves as persons: They had developed into a 'community of learners'.

The Community of Learners as a Medium for Knowledge Generation

Analyzing the group work as cycles of learning, highlights the process rather than the product. My next step was to approach the group learning as a means of knowledge generation; of achieving new understanding. I returned to the double locus model from a new angle, in which I related to the two contexts as two forms of *teachers' knowing.* (Fenstermacher 1994)

Fenstermacher distinguishes between two forms of teachers' knowing stemming from two different mode of inquiry: practical inquiry within the classroom, which yields teacher knowledge/practical (TK/P), and the more formal inquiry, which characterizes the social reflective context, yielding teacher knowledge/formal (TK/F).

The interplay or tension between these two contexts, or modes of inquiry, is, in my view, critical for the process of reconstructing knowledge, and for building new teaching and learning theories. It is the facilitator's responsibility to create this tension in such a setting by probing and teasing out reflection or self-inquiry, and eliciting from the teachers the kind of knowledge-in-action that is tacit in nature. Without this kind of a dialogue, there is little chance of breeding alternative ideas, or alternative stories. In my view, the facilitator should be more actively involved in the dialogue in order to enable both parties to actually "share each other's castles". His or her task is to help the teachers move between the two types of inquiry.

This interplay brought me back to Kolb and Fry's concept of 'dialectical tension' (introduced in Chapter 2), a tension that exists between different components of experiential learning. A dialectical tension between here-and-now experience and theoretical conceptualization, and between active experimentation and reflective observation, stimulates the learning process and enhances mutual learning (see Figure 6.1).

Fielding (1996) refers to Kolb and Fry's model, in terms of different modes of learning, showing that participants in a heterogeneous learning group, can be viewed as representing these four preferred styles of learning. (Fielding 1995)

Assuming that in the STES collaborative group, the teachers' preferred form of inquiry or learning is practical, based on here-and-now experience, and that the researchers' form of inquiry or preferred learning is formal, implying more abstract conceptualization, these components could serve as criteria for analysis. In other words, we could use them to trace the interplay between the teachers' and researchers' roles in the generation of new understanding or new theories.

Figure 6.1: Kolb and Fry Model of Experiential Learning

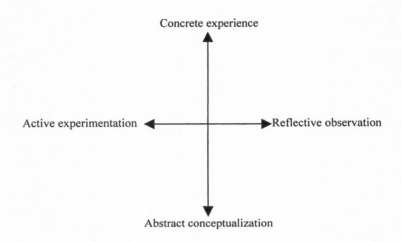

The following excerpts taken from the group discourse serve to trace this interplay:

The 20th group meeting (12.3.1995)

The explicit aim of the STES project was to develop curriculum units that would broaden awareness of and responsibility for real social and environmental problems. A meeting had been scheduled for the following month for all of the other teams who took part in the project, and each group of teachers was asked to prepare a general plan of their curriculum module for presentation.

This formed the background to my opening words at the meeting, asking the participants for suggestions as to how to prepare our presentation of "Desert and Desertification".

Hava: - I see no problem. All our classroom activities are recorded. We can hand over the list.

Edna: - We can pick some major issues which have been discussed here, and examine how, or to what extent they were dealt with in the classroom.

These two responses illustrate two different orientations of curriculum development. The teacher's orientation is clearly concrete, whereas the researcher's orientation is more abstract and reflective. In terms of the curriculum model, the teacher's implicit model is prescriptive, whereas the researcher's model is reflexive.

The 22nd group meeting (19.3.1995)

The meeting was opened by Hava inviting the group to participate in a student conference the following Monday. The idea of the conference goes back to the group decisions concerning key issues that had been neglected, such as 'desertification'.

Moti, one of the scientific researchers, was invited to give a talk on the subject. However, Hava, the leading teacher, had a different agenda for the conference; to help the students with their individual projects. These conflicting aims are conveyed in the following excerpt:

Moti: - I understood that the point was 'desertification'.

Oren: - It is pertinent to convene now, before the end of term vacation, and help disperse the fog, leaving them feeling better with respect to the projects. I suggest we open the conference with a lecture on desertification.

Moti agrees to open the topic of desertification for discussion. He resents the idea of a lecture:

Moti: - I am concerned with the fact that their projects do not relate to the time dimension, but rather convey the here–and–now. I am disturbed by the fact that they are focused on the classical static orientation, completely unaware of the dynamics of change. That is why I am keen on deliberating on the key concept,

'Desertification', which, as a dynamic concept could open questions, such as:
Is desertification a negative or a positive process?
Is it a natural cyclic process or rather man made?
How does external inteference such as provision of food and medication, inhibit natural processes?

Orna: - It reminds me of a film, The Politics of Hunger, which deals with the so-called aid that the western countries offer, for example, in the periodical dry seasons in the Sahal region in Western Africa. These are real ethical questions. To what extent do the huge food transports actually help the local population or, paradoxically, do they result in perpetuating the situation, by limiting local initiatives?

Hava: - It sounds exciting and most important. However, I would like to dedicate the day to their personal projects. I suggest we ask them to report on where they stand and what kind of help they need, and from there, arrive at desertification.

Moti opened the issue of desertification at the students' conference, as planned. The discussion that developed was most stimulating, eliciting the students' active participation. The teachers were content, admitting that it succeeded in opening up many new aspects and venues of thought, as well as real ethical questions.

Apart from the struggle between the parties over who controlled the students' learning process, the above excerpt illustrates the tension between the two opposing orientations: the concrete here-and-now situation, of reacting to the students' perceived needs, and the researchers' desire to function on a more abstract, conceptual level of learning.

The 24th group meeting (30.4.1995)

The meeting took place soon after the STES project meeting of all the developing groups of teachers. Meeting with different teams, who presented various drafts of curricular modules, gave our teachers a broader perspective regarding their task as curriculum developers and their obligation to produce the module.

Moti: - I see this as a stage of evaluation, yet how can we evaluate our work before the students' projects are submitted?

Edna: - I would like to draw a distinction between evaluation and curriculum development. We began with no real curriculum, only ambiguous ideas and a list of aims. Today, retrospectively, we are in a position to write it down. The class can be seen as an experiential site, where we test our work and find out the extent to which we actually reach our aims.

Moti: - You mean that the curriculum module we develop, would reflect what we actually did here?

Moti's first comments about evaluation reflect a rather linear Tylerian conception of a curriculum. In comparison, Edna introduces a dynamic, more circular or system concept, which is action-research oriented and according to which, the classroom is seen as a medium for testing teaching activities and their congruence with the curricular manifested aims. This idea is then picked up by another researcher, who rephrases it in different terms:

Ruth: - I agree. It's the working principles that we have to extract in order to produce the curriculum module, which can be ready for repeated experimentation. By implementing it again, whether by our teachers or by others, we can test the applicability of these principles.

Ruth's new concept of 'working principles' emphasizes the idea already mentioned, of theoretical constructs, which are extracted from the classroom experience, in other words the rationale of the developing curricular module. I see this as an illustration of Kolb and Fry's abstract conceptualization, the researchers preferred mode of inquiry, or mode of learning. In terms of curriculum development, it portrays an action-research orientation.

The teachers' reaction is reflected in the following excerpt:

Hava: - In order to produce a curricular module for another teacher to use, we have to state the rationale and give a few examples for him to apply. We have no interest in producing a cook-book of the kind that I saw some other STES groups develop.

Dan: - I am not afraid of a curriculum framework; a curriculum is not
necessarily a cook-book.
Oren: - By formulating a curriculum module, we will fall into the pit
that we wanted to avoid...our aim was to create a breakthrough...
Dan: - But even an open-school has a curriculum...

This short excerpt exhibits the teachers' different ideas of the
curriculum. To remind the reader, the whole idea of developing
"Desert and Desertification" as a new curriculum, sprung from
their deep frustration of the existing curriculum, and their joint
desire to create a breakthrough. Yet it seemed to me that both
Hava and Oren were still very much anchored in the classical
idea of a highly structured curriculum (a cookbook) from which
they desperately wanted to break out. I see their suggestion of a
module that contains the rationale plus examples for the teacher
to follow, albeit unstructured, as essentially not much different
from the prescribed type of curriculum. Dan seems less
entrapped by the classical concept of the curriculum and,
therefore, he is not afraid to use the term. This indicates to me
that he has reconstructed the concept of curriculum, so that it
now includes a much broader idea, such as that of an open-school
curriculum.

Saar: - When I come to think of it, the students were pressed to
choose their topics before we exposed them to the wider aspects of
the issue, or the desert. One of our conclusions today, could be to
expose them before they have to make their choice of topic.
Facilitator: - This is a good example to our method of curriculum
development, how to extract from our experience a few principles,
such as the one suggested by Saar. Another example relates to the
landscape sculptor. His activity was subject to our reflection and
deliberation. Today, we have to rationalize the activity. What goal
did it serve? We cannot just issue a recipe: "Invite a sculptor".

Saar voices his own grappling with this new idea of working
principles, or extracting constructs from classroom experience.
By using an example, he is able to illustrate the process. My
response, which serves to elaborate the idea, illustrates the role of
the facilitator, as I understand it. This is an example of what I
mean by oscillating between the two modes of learning, using

concrete examples to explain abstract theoretical constructs and, thus, engage the teachers in a more formal mode of learning.
A new aspect of the curriculum is introduced in the discourse:

Avi: - It is pertinent for us to find a way how to advertise our work, not merely as something unique, carried out in a unique setting. Every curriculum stems from an ideology. Our ideology should form the framework, the underlying basis of our curriculum.

Aviva: - I see the importance of developing a curriculum module mainly in terms of our own benefit, for achieving a better understanding of what we do here.

Saar: - I have no interest in an esoteric curriculum unless it is of value beyond our local experience. One of our groups' main messages, as well as that of the Internet, is that there are different methods of collecting information, of attaining knowledge, and that it is our job to prepare our students accordingly. This I see as the main message of our curriculum unit. We have to show how it can be done.

This last part of the discourse touches on the moral aspect of the curriculum, what Avi calls the curriculum ideology. For the module to be applicable to other teachers, its underlying ideology needs to be clearly formulated (in our case the STES rationale). Aviva, from her practical point of reference, emphasizes the teacher's need to understand better, as her main incentive for participating in such a curriculum development process. Saar brings the discussion to closure, tying up the whole groups' endeavor with its sound logical as well as moral rationale.

Kolb and Fry's dialectical tension, helped me to better understand the nature of the collaborative group and the function played by the different participants. I believe this analysis justified my rather intuitive idea of the heterogeneity of the group as a means of enhancing and stimulating the groups' self-inquiry, its learning process.

Apart from Orna (who was a curriculum developer), the researchers who participated in the group had no formal knowledge of education. Yet, their formal theoretical mode of inquiry helped to create the dialectical tension with the teachers' more practical mode of thinking and conceptualizing. This does not imply that teachers were not able to engage in theoretical abstract conceptualization. My main argument is that within their school context (as a 'landscape' that transmit 'sacred stories' embedded in the positivistic underlying conception of the school system), they tend to function instrumentally; in other words, to conceive their role in terms of transmitting curricular knowledge.

The impact is so strong that even in this non-conventional high school for environmental education, and with this group of creative innovating teachers, their plan of a new curriculum did not seem to have the wings to actually create the desired breakthrough.

Similar examples are to be found in different countries all over the world: innovations, for example, connected to the introduction of computers into the school, and the use of new information sources, such as the Internet. Many such innovative ideas generated by the teachers, do not achieve the expected breakthrough. The bottom line is that no real change can be achieved without the necessary conceptual change that teachers as well as researchers and administrators have to undergo, to liberate themselves from the dominating 'sacred stories' and allow them to create multiple alternative stories.

Discussion

I began the project with the idea of a learning community consisting of a diverse group of people able to maintain an egalitarian relationship by respecting each other as professionals. The participant teachers were all experienced and, in many respects, experts in their profession. The researchers were more heterogeneous in age, status and experience, ranging from senior researchers to graduate students. I saw this heterogeneous group as an optimal medium to enhance inquiry, deliberation and reflection; a medium that enables its participants to express themselves as persons. Establishing a 'community of learners' within the STES framework which consists an Internet as a new way of knowledge search, I believed we could achieve a breakthrough in terms of knowledge. In other words, *extend the concept of knowledge* to include experiential, authentic, and subjective knowledge; multifaceted knowledge such as that derived from problem-solving processes, open to different interpretations; knowledge that is not neutral but value laden.

In fact, the extension of the concept of knowledge turned out to be the main achievement of the project. It required a whole year's work to achieve the teachers' manifested guiding principle namely, " Exposure of the students to different aspects of the issue, to alternative sources of knowledge and different ways of data collection".

Beyond these expected outcomes, some important unexpected perspectives were achieved. All participants gained a deeper under-standing of the following points:

a) Curriculum as a process rather than content

"Desert and Desertification" was to be published as a formal curricular module for STS teaching in high schools. One of the main concerns of the developing team was to preserve its unique educational orientation. "How to ensure that the next team of teachers would not turn the module into a textbook and use it to transmit knowledge in the conventional frontal classroom?" was an issue constantly discussed. I believe that it reflects the teachers' newly acquired concept of *curriculum as a process*, a process of mutual learning of teachers and students, as compared to curriculum as *content,* that is, a package of learning materials to be transmitted to the students.

b) A new Action Research model for School-Based-Curriculum-Development (SBCD)

The process of curriculum development within the community of learners, differs from the conventional SBCD, based on the Tylerian model.   Instead of formulating objectives and translating them into learning activities, our case study represents a reverse process, one that begins with (often intuitive) practice. By reflecting on their actions, the teachers were able to disclose underlying assumptions and then conceptualize their experience into educational principles. This is what we termed an action-research model of curriculum development.   This model is reflective rather than didactic, involving circular rather than linear thinking, and it is based on the ecological or cybernetic rather than positivistic orientation.

c) The interactive double loci model as a framework for professional development.

While indulging in STES curriculum development, the participants undergo a process of conceptual change. This applies not only to the teachers, but to all participants of the community of learners. Researchers, community–people, parents and educational administrators, all move from the positivistic towards the cybernetic or ecological orientation.

d) Teachers as learners

In conclusion, to change their pedagogical orientation, teachers have to become learners. In other words, they have to indulge in inquiry learning, preferably within Action Research settings, regarding it as a prerequisite for moving from teaching to learning. This goal of *turning the teachers into learners.* was only partly achieved in the first year of the STES project. This is no trivial change, nor is it easily attained. It implies using their reflective capacities to learn from their practice and formalize their theories of action. It means generating or reconstructing professional knowledge dealing with ways to promote their students' learning and to orchestrate the classroom as a 'community of learners'.

Chapter 7

Ecological Thinking

I opened this book by introducing the metaphor of *ecological thinking* as alternative approach to educational change. This is my term for the 'new thinking' that I believe should replace current linear thinking in education. Based on circular causality, reflexivity and self-organization, ecological thinking connotes a new notion of learning, teaching, curriculum, and the role of the teacher, as well as a new conception of educational change.

The notion of ecological thinking (ET) emerged from my interaction with the field of practice. Other terms have been mentioned in the book, such as 'system thinking,' 'cybernetics' and more specifically, 'second-order cybernetics'. It took me more than two decades of research to arrive at the notion of ecological thinking. In this chapter, I justify my choice of this new term and show its advantages over other, similar terms.

My conception of 'ecological thinking' is influenced by the modern ecological conception of 'open systems,' whereby humans are not regarded as 'disturbances' of the ecological equilibrium, but as important components of ecological systems (Davis 1986). Thus, ET relates to the double role that we humans play, as both actors and reflectors. As *actors,* they interact with the other components of the system, and as *reflectors,* they are aware of the system and themselves as interactive within it and, therefore, that they are responsible for their own understanding and their actions.   In this respect, ecological thinking is almost synonymous to 'second-order cybernetics', which can be defined as the state of "including in one's observations oneself as an observer too" (Foerster 1992). However, I hope to be able to demonstrate the differences between the two concepts, in order to justify my new approach to educational change.

My prior attempts to put forward this notion of educational thinking have taught me to prefer concrete examples to theoretical deliberation; examples of self-organizing frameworks in which both the process and product of ecological thinking develop.   In the following, I go back to the field of practice to select case studies that demonstrate the process of ET as a dialogic discourse within a 'community of learners', and ET as the emergent product.

My first case study is taken from the Shalom [Peace] School, the only high school in Mitzpeh-Ramon, a small town in the desert.

A Case Study of an Urban System

Mizpeh-Ramon is a small town of five thousand inhabitants, built on the rim of the Ramon crater in the Negev desert. Overlooking an amazingly picturesque landscape, it forms part of the Ramon Nature Reserve Park.   The small size of the town and its accessibility to its physical environment, make it an optimal field for developing a curriculum dealing with Man-environment relationship.

The idea was to develop an inquiry-based curriculum unit, requiring students to start by investigating their own urban system and then gradually enlarge the scale to include larger physical and human systems, indeed, the whole biosphere.   The aim of the curriculum was to develop the students' awareness of the mutual relationship between humans and their environment, and their responsibility to act wisely.

As part of her Ph D thesis, Noa, who actually lived in Mizpeh Ramon, met regularly with an interdisciplinary group of the school's teachers, all of whom were committed to the idea of developing the new curricular approach. A 10th grade classroom was chosen as the experiential site for the new curricular ideas to be practiced (see our double-locus model in Chapter 5). The deliberations of both learning sites, the classroom and the teachers' regular weekly meetings, were recorded, transcribed and distributed among all participants. Thus, the group was, in fact, practicing action-research.

The teachers began the process by asking the students to choose a problem in their urban reality, in their every-day encounters with their town, and turn it into a research study. To their great surprise, the students' reaction was apatheric. They showed complete lack of interest, claiming they were too well acquainted with their town, and saw no sense in inquiring into the known.

Reflecting over the issue in their weekly meeting, the teachers decided to reverse their course of action and start from the abstract rather than the concrete. They decided to teach systems by first introducing a simple closed ecological system and then gradually moving on to more complicated open human systems. To practice this new deductive orien-tation, each of the teacher participants in the group chose an example of a system. Common criteria were then extracted from these examples, which helped them define what they meant by a system, and one teacher volunteered to teach 'systems.'

The students' reaction was passive and non-cooperative, their interest diminished from one period to the next. In a general discussion of students and teachers, the students voiced their feeling of boredom. The teachers interpreted this as an indication of the students' difficulty to cope with abstract complex learning.

In an effort to better understand this frustrating learning situation, the group used the semester break for intensive meetings and dialectical reflection on their own action.
The following excerpt is taken from their group discussion (4.1.2000):

- We seem to be failing them somehow...
- The presence of the principal affected the students' behavior.
- I believe that the students are also to blame. They lack even a minimum of tolerance and commitment. I think we are entitled to some kind of mutual respect...

- I assumed that being highly antagonistic towards the formal educational system, they would appreciate this unique project. But the same attitude prevailed here.
- They identify it as irrelevant.
- We are trying a new way that requires high commitment on their part and they are not able to meet our demands.
- I don't like the idea of our role being to 'entertain' our students.
- We presented a clear schedule, stating that our aims were to explore our urban system, to acquire research tools and altogether, to regard them as partners...
- I suggest we find another group that might be more interested.
- OK, but how do we ensure that the new group will be seriously committed?
- I am optimistic. Once we find a group that is basically tolerant to new ideas, and give them the space to choose their line of inquiry, we will capture their interest and achieve collaboration.

The school principal was interviewed and his narrative was triangulated with the group discourse. As a result, some important reasons for failure were highlighted:

* Bad choice of class.
* School system is oriented toward short-term achievements, usually by testing.
* Students are socialized to the conventional teaching model of knowledge transmission.
* Lack of tolerance to ambiguity, uncertainty.
* As teachers, we ourselves were not clear enough.

By reflecting on their findings, the group managed to formulate the following guidelines for further planning:

* Individual inquiry has to be experienced; it cannot be explained.
* Teachers have to be exposed themselves to the inquiry field before teaching it.
* They have to be open to challenges.
* Our group as a 'democratic space' is of vast importance for our mutual learning process.

Their joint decision was to apply a concrete inductive process of inquiry rather than continue deductively and, starting with a new class, expose the students to a new unknown urban system.

The choice fell on the shopping mall of Beer-Sheva, the capital city of the Negev some 50 miles north of Mitzpeh-Ramon. The mall, which is known as a favorite place for the local youth, would serve as a case study of a complex system.

In their first classroom activity, the students were requested to generate questions about the mall: "What were they interested to know?" "What did they want to learn about the mall?" Much to the teachers' surprise, long lists of questions were produced. However, on closer examination, most of them were found to be simple, informational and closed questions.

For example (from the group meeting on 2.2.2000)

- Who is responsible for the lights in the mall?
- What is the role of the head manager? How does he start his day?
- Which are the most crowded days at the mall?
- Which is the most profitable shop?

The main issue to be discussed at the next meeting was 'how to teach their students to generate more complex, open-ended questions, questions that could initiate the inquiry process.'

A little scaffolding was needed for the students to classify questions according to different levels of complexity and to generate focal interdisciplinary value-laden questions, questions that stem from their personal conceptual field. For example:

- What makes the mall so profitable?
- What is the advantage of a mall over regular high-street business?

With these new focal questions, they divided into teams, each choosing a research question.

A visit to the mall was planned one afternoon. The students' assignment was to collect information in order to deal with their specific questions. They were instructed to seek out different sources of information, by observing, interviewing, and questioning people, reading material, etc. They were active and highly motivated, collecting relevant data within their teams. The teachers' only help was to schedule interviews with key figures identified by the students, and to escort them to their various meetings. Altogether, the visit was enjoyable as well as highly productive in terms of learning. As each team reported its findings in the classroom, the complexity of the mall as a system, the numerous interrelations between its subsystems, were revealed.

The next assignment was to draw a model of the mall as a system. Figures 7.1, 7.2 depict the students' models. Viewing the models as an indication of the students' conception of a system, the teachers were pleased to note that they all revealed complexity, consisting of various different factors and showing inter-connectedness between the different components; some even suggested dynamism as a dimension of change.

It took a while for the teachers to realize what was missing in the students' models, and their conception of a system: All of the teams had designed the mall as a closed system, independent of 'outsiders' – the consumers. Model 7.2 had the consumers at the bottom of the hierarchy, indicating that the mall's products were eventually purchased by buyers. However, the fact that consumers were the target population, influencing, directly or indirectly the mall's various functions, was absent. There was no indication of the potential crowds of visitors, including themselves, as operators.

Opening with a question, "What is missing in the models?" the teachers lead a most significant classroom discussion. Gradually, ideas and suggestions were aired and thrashed out, and a new model was jointly constructed (see Figures 7.3).

Figure 7.1: A model of the Mall as a system

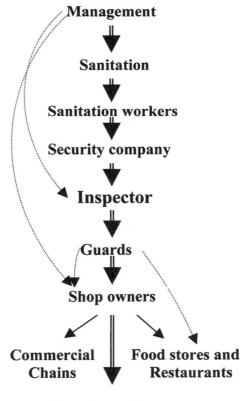

Figure 7.2: **A model of the Mall as a system**

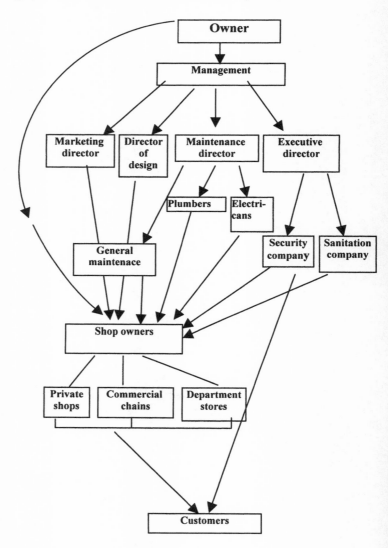

This case study illustrates the process of developing ecological thinking of the teachers and their students.

A new learning framework was introduced which met with the students' resistance. As a reaction, the teachers reverted to didactic teaching. Having changed their teaching framework from disciplinary to interdisciplinary, from one teacher in a classroom, to teamwork, it seemed that *they had not changed their role conception*, as they were still adhering to the conventional model of transmitting knowledge. Moreover, they seemed insensitive to their students' real needs or interests, and instead of analyzing what went wrong and why, they tended to blame the students' inability to cope with abstract issues.

Although they had created a collaborative framework of weekly meetings, this was not used by the teachers to venture deeper and question their basic assumptions about knowledge, learning, and the teacher's role. In other words, they failed to develop as a 'community of learners'.

The turning point was in the semester break, which was dedicated to serious critical reflection. During this time, new insights were generated and some of the teachers' entrenched assumptions were disclosed, for example, regarding the prevailing school culture and its effect on students' attitudes and behavior. They became aware of their own limitations (not having themselves practiced the new way) and hence, their uncertainty about how to act. Awareness of the importance of their group meetings as a learning context signified meta-learning.

The activity in the shopping mall clearly illustrates the mutuality of the two learning contexts. The teachers initiate the process by exposing the students to the mall system, asking them to generate questions. The students' responses, which indicate their ability to generate questions, effect (or 'teach') their teachers. The teachers' basic assumptions about the students' lack of motivation and inability to learn or ask questions, undergoes change. A mutual learning process of this kind can be likened to two cogwheels rotating each other.

The most significant part of their mutual learning was around the construction of a model of a system. The students' first attempts (Figures 7.1 and 7.2) helped the teachers draw the distinction between closed and open systems. The teachers' further probing questions served as scaffolds for their students' new understanding.

Figure 7.3: A joint class model of the Mall as a system

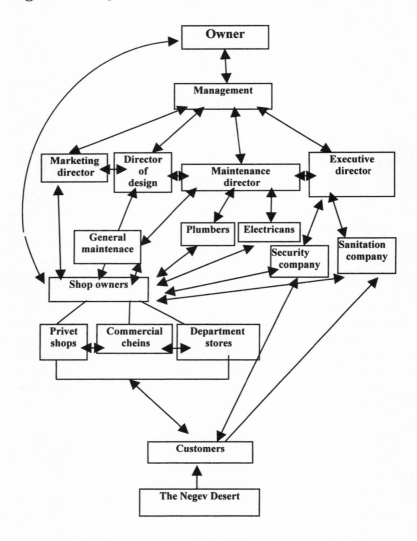

Thus, students learned by exploring the field, in this case, an urban system. The teachers learned through their students' process of inquiry. They also learned how to orchestrate this new type of classroom activity. That is they learned to act as constructivist teachers whose role is to enhance their students' ability to act as responsible autonomous learners, as both actors and reflectors.

In terms of ecological thinking, both parties learned to be interactive insiders as well as reflective outsiders by conceptualizing their learning (meta-learning) into theories (or models) of action.

Second Case Study: Evaluating the STES Curriculum Module

Our second case is about a collaborative group of nine teachers from 'Tzafit,' a regional comprehensive school 50 miles north of Beer-Sheva, who participated in the STES project. Two educational researchers acted as facilitators. A 10th grade classroom was allotted as the initial site for practicing the STES curriculum for three periods a week. Three out of the nine teachers chose to act as experiential teachers. The choice to participate in the experiment was given to the students, too: They could choose between STES and Biology.

The group as a whole met regularly every other week, forming a medium for reflection and gradually developing as a 'community of learners'. Their explicit task was to develop an interdisciplinary, inquiry-oriented student-centered curriculum unit, which they called, "Progress as tension between a blessing and a curse". The title reflected a 'hot' issue defined in terms of a moral dilemma.

The group held 26 meetings during the school year. All proceedings were audiotaped, transcribed and distributed among the participants. These transcripts also served as our database for the analysis of the group discourse.

From the outset, the team had difficulty in trying to evaluate their students' learning process, as well as its products or achievements. They realized (at first intuitively) that their conventional way of evaluating and grading would not fit the new STES pedagogy, which required students in teams to choose their topics of study. Moreover, focusing on authentic moral dilemmas concerning progress in society put the teachers in a completely new situation. Compared to the conventional school curriculum, designed to teach the already known, the teachers in our case could not predict the products.

As facilitators of the process, we decided to pick this issue of evaluation and follow up its development in the group discourse as an indicator of the group's process of learning.

Following the Group's Process of Learning

Part I: Assessing the students' work

The first questions about evaluation arose two months after the beginning of school year (13.11.97): "How to evaluate the students' work".

Amalia: - I'm a little uneasy about team work. How can we assess each student's individual achievement within the team?

Kochi: - I've given them files for their work-sheets. These could also serve as drafts for evaluation.

Shosh: - Say I was your student. How would you grade my work?

Amalia: - I'll think of a way by the time I have to give them marks.

Shosh: - Maybe the main idea of the drafts is to enable us follow the students' work.

It is evident that the group participants are acting as *outsiders* in the process: They need to assess their students' progress as well as their products but, as teachers, they don't see themselves as part of the process. They see their role as knowers, as transmitters of knowledge, and the students, as learners.

The group's idea of a portfolio (drafts) as a means of evaluation highlights two points: (a) It enables teachers to follow the work of each student in order to assess his/her learning.   b) It enables the teachers to read the qualitative changes that take place at each stage by conceptualizing them as indicators of better understanding of the whole learning process.

This second type of evaluation 'through the process' (Bernstein, 1996) implies evaluating the curriculum; a process of curriculum evaluation, which puts the teachers within the process as *insiders*. Yet, there is no indication in the above excerpt that the teachers regarded the portfolios as a means for evaluating the curriculum.

Two weeks later (27.11.97) the issue of evaluation is raised again, in conjunction with Parents-Day, when teachers report to the parents on the progress of their offspring.

Kochi: - Before Parents-Day, I collected all their worksheets. From that moment on, they understood that we were serious, and that this is a curriculum just like any other curriculum. They asked me to give marks but I refused. Some students fail to take STES seriously. We will have to talk to them together with their parents.

Kochi refuses to mark their drafts. He is concerned about the learning process; but the students are concerned about their marks. It is evident that each party assigns a different meaning to evaluation. Kochi's idea of the STES curriculum is *process-oriented,* whereas the students' is *product-oriented.*

As an insider, Kochi is confronted with a new constraint, the 'school culture'. For over 10 years, the students have been socialized to believe that every important task deserves a mark. Their interpretation of an unmarked assignment is, that this work is not important enough. Confused, Kochi reverts back to the old 'solutions.'

Shosh: - When we are faced by difficulties, such as giving marks or lack of responsibility, we run back to the known methods, talking with the parents... That's not what we wanted. We were aiming at arousing their internal motivation.

She is reflecting on the complexity of the evaluative situation. She also warns against regressing back to conventional patterns of punishment...

To sum up this first part, the group comes to distinguish between the product and the process of learning; between assessing the individual student's progress and evaluating the curriculum, and between their role as outsiders and as insiders. Intuitively, the teachers sense that the drafts are no more than products, but they have no other tools for tracing the students' process of learning.

These initial events reflect the difficulties teachers have to face when they choose to practice a new pedagogy; the pressures, both external and internal, that they have to confront.

Part II: Conceptualizing practice.

As part of the larger STES project, which ran in three different universities (see Chapter 6), our group was asked to prepare a poster of our curriculum module and to present it at a general meeting. For this purpose, the group divided into sub-teams and, in the next group meeting, each presented a different idea.

The following is a description of the metaphor produced by one of the sub-teams:

Tzvia and Shlomo: - We drew a labyrinth. Labyrinth, to us, conveys a sense of 'not knowing' what is going on. There is one entrance for the students and the teacher, and they are together in the labyrinth. At first, I thought there was only one exit. Then I understood there were many exits.

Amalia: - Why should a student want to enter the labyrinth in the first place?

Shlomo: - The labyrinth symbolizes 'progress'. We enter whether we want to or not. We walk along an unknown path. We do not know where it leads to.

Tzvia: - These are things we have to write down and clarify.

Batia: - It makes sense. We don't know where we are going.

The metaphor of 'labyrinth' is used here to symbolize both 'progress' and the main idea of the curriculum. Instead of one exit (the traditional-conventional educational process), there are many exits (different processes, different outcomes). Thus, the team deals with the curriculum as a whole, trying to conceptualize their practice and reconstruct new curriculum knowledge.

Moreover, the exercise reflects learning as 'participation', as a process that occurs in a 'community of learners', within a discourse or new language, which also forms their identity (Sfard 1998). The teachers act here as learners. In an attempt to verbalize their practice, they feel there are things we have to write down and clarify.

Their next decision was to try this same exercise with their students.

In the next group meeting (11.12.97), they present the students' reports; their images of the curriculum module:

- The first student team drew a boy describing the curriculum, learning in natural surroundings, and asking a lot of questions about what we see.
- The second team wrote: "We learn to think, we learn different ways of work, we learn to listen, we learn reading comprehension, and we also learn to talk, to present and transmit what we are doing".
- The third team tried to present the curriculum graphically, by drawing human evolution from the monkey to Homo Sapiens.

Different levels of conceptualization are represented in the students' images: The first image relates to the level of *conditions of the new learning* (natural environment and asking questions); the second, to the level of *the meaning of learning,* by specifying what the process of learning meant to them: thinking; listening; talking; transmitting; different ways of working; the third, relates to the level of *change and development* by referring to human development (a process whose outcomes are unpredictable).

The teachers' suggestion to use their students' ideas or images signified a new approach: They now regard the students as co-learners. As a result of this new collaboration, a highly multifaceted image of the module is achieved. It seems as if the students have provided the evidence to substantiate the teacher's labyrinth metaphor: "a curriculum that initiates many different processes, as well as many different outcomes".

To sum up, this second part depicts a shift from intuitive to conceptual thinking. Collaboration with students in the sense of mutual learning implies that they have become insiders, part of the 'community of learners'.

Part III: The emergence of new understanding

Evaluation of the curriculum was the topic of another group meeting (14.5.98)

Batia: - Our main didactic goal was to find ways to develop the students to become young researchers. I would like to examine whether we achieved this goal.
(and a little later)
- Next year, we have to be clearer about our expected outcomes: the inter-mediate stages of evaluation, the degree of freedom, etc. By not asse-ssing their work in the middle of the year, we nearly lost them.

Here evaluation is seen as an assessment process, controlled by predetermined goals and objectives. Batia is reflecting retrospectively on what has been done, and prospectively on what should be done. Later, during the same meeting:

Kochi: -   One of the most valuable things our students have experienced, is the fact that different teachers, from different subject areas, disagree on many issues. Moreover, their different points of view were openly discussed in the classroom. They stopped acting as teachers in front of their students, and just acted as themselves. Our students felt as if they were part of something new.
Shlomo: - For me, the whole learning process was very different from any other teaching situation. For example, my prior knowledge on 'quality of life' was no more than that of the students, which was not much... I experienced a process of learning just like the students.

A different model of evaluation is reflected, whereby the achievement described were not predefined. This new model *emerged* from the process, surprising the teachers no less than the students. Here we had a completely new pedagogy, based on knowledge that does not represent a one-and-only truth, and on the teacher as participant learner rather than transmitter of knowledge.

To sum up, we chose to follow the evolution of the concept 'evaluation' as an indication of the group process of professional development, that is, ecological thinking. At the beginning (Part I), the teacher participants understand evaluation in terms of assessing their students' learning, emphasizing the product rather than the process. On the other hand, their view of the portfolio as means of evaluating the whole process, through the process, shows that they are also inside actors.

In Part II, participants begin to conceptualize their practice by reflecting on their action. They collaborate with their students in a mutual learning setting, thus reflecting a shift in their role conception. As interactive learners, they are insiders as well as reflective outsiders. At this stage, evaluation is seen not merely as a process of students' assessment but also of curriculum evaluation.

Finally, in Part III, curriculum evaluation is no longer understood in terms of Tyler's predetermined objectives, and a new model emerges, a reflective model based on action-research. The group functions as a 'community of learners', constructing new understanding. As such, they are interactive insiders and reflective outsiders, able to reflect and to conceptualize their theories of action.

Third Case Study: Constructing a Core Curriculum

Chronologically, this case study, taken from Tzafit regional compre-hensive school (introduced in the above case study), was two years later. A new school principal had been appointed. Highly impressed by the pedagogy that emerged from the STES project, he threw out a challenge:

> - I want to move our focus from teaching to learning; to transform the school curriculum from a conventional teaching-oriented curriculum into one that is centered on students' autonomous learning.

Accordingly, a team was formed, consisting of the principal and several leading teachers, and I was asked to act as facilitator.

In the first meetings, the team defined its task in terms of developing a core curriculum for the whole junior high school.

Central themes were chosen for each of the three grades (7th-9th), as 'umbrella topics' for students' individual or team inquiry studies.

This team, which met regularly for two school years, gradually developed into a 'community of learners'. All proceedings were recorded, transcribed, and copies were distributed among the participants for further reflection. Selected excerpts from the group discourse will serve to follow the mutual learning process of the group.

One of the first topics of discussion was "Family Roots", the central theme for the 7th grade individual inquiry studies. The following excerpt was taken from one of the first group meetings:

Uri: - The "family roots" study misses the point. It does not fit our idea of a research project.

Jonathan (the Head): - The idea is that each student will conduct an inquiry into his own family.

Uri: - I see "family roots" as a strong personal experience. I would like them to stay there, instead of turning it into a research study ... to sit with their mother over a cup of coffee and listen to her stories.

Shosh: - The question is what do we mean by a research study?

Uri: - I have worked with kids on individual research studies. I gave them an instruction sheet and explained the assignment item by item, took them to the library, and followed up the whole process.

Two models of 'research study' emerge in the discourse: the empirical scientific versus the naturalistic, ethnographic or interpretive model. Uri, a history teacher who has gained experience in scientifically oriented research studies, cannot accept family stories as data. Moreover, he is afraid of spoiling authentic family experiences by turning them into a study assignment. At this point, it seems that Uri is voicing the group's research orientation because no contradictory comments are raised.

The following excerpt, taken from the next group meeting, deals with 'teamwork'. It relates to the 8th grade study topic, which was to be carried out in teams. The group discussion stemmed from the question: "What do we mean by team-learning?"

Shosh: - Are we clear about what we mean by teamwork?
Uri: - First we have to construct criteria. The group then generates questions and decide, together, on one research question. Roles are then negotiated, and the process is mapped. The same criteria could serve also as criteria of evaluation.
Judith: - I believe that our work here as a team illustrates what we mean by teamwork.
Shosh: - Could we extract criteria from this group meeting, for example?
Uri: - I feel great about the way we listen to each other, sharing each others' problems....
Irit: - To me, the most important issue is being connected to the real needs of the school.

Again we are confronted by two different ideas of teamwork. The first reflects a didactic orientation, whereby the teacher instructs the students how to work in a team; the second, a reflexive orientation, whereby principles of group work are identified and conceptualized *from* our own practical experience. A confrontation between the two could trigger the participants' reflection on their underlying basic assumptions. Instead, there is a turn in the conversation from the cognitive to a more affective dimension; from teamwork as a topic of conversation, to *how we feel within our own teamwork in the group*. The facilitating climate of sharing, caring and togetherness, which characterize the context of learning, is openly expressed. Park termed this type of discourse 'relational knowledge', knowledge that unites the knower and the known as an outcome of the interaction (Park 1999, Gorodetsky and Keiny 2002).

Some of the teacher participants in the group were also involved in the experiential part of the project; they could use the new ideas generated in the team and try them out experientially in their field of practice (see Figure 1.1). The following excerpt, which was taken from a group meeting about two months later, deals with the question of how to conduct an inquiry study in the classroom.

Elisheva: - How does a teacher cope with a classroom of 35 kids and, at the same time, manage individual or team inquiry studies?

Uri: - I want to share with you my experience in my 7th grade classroom where I teach both History and "Family Roots". I shall start with History. I opened the lesson by saying, I don't feel like teaching you; you teach me. What a commotion I caused! They started talking about forming teams. I asked them, "How do you divide into teams?

They threw out some ideas ... criteria ... Teams were formed and they sat together, negotiating how to plan their work. One team wrote down: "What do we want to know from this particular chapter?" "How, in what way, are we going to present it in the classroom?" This was a new experience for me, and that is how I approached my second task, "Family Roots". I told them that I do not feel like teaching the way I did in the past, then drew a circle on the board, and wrote 'Roots' in the middle. "What do we do now?" I asked. "Add my name to the circle", responded one boy. "Why?" I asked, "Because the study begins with me".

I handed pages around and everyone added their name to the circle. "What now?" "Extend the family". This started a discussion on who should be included and who shouldn't. One boy commented, "I have a problem. My grandfather was killed in Kurdistan, and my grandmother cannot talk about it".

A girl joins in: "I have a similar problem. I lost my brother when I was 5 years old, but when I wrote a poem about him, my father was deeply hurt..." Many more joined in the conversation, throwing out suggestions, raising more problems...

Neomi: - What did it do to you?

Uri: - From an inquiry study activity it turned into ethical or rather, 'value education'.

Uri's monologue, compared to his previous argumentation at the beginning of our work, evidently reflects his conceptual change. It seems that he has travelled a long way since he defended his model of research study against the more personal ethnographic model, and he has managed to resolve the gap between the two. Simultaneously, the group, too, has developed from simple collaboration towards a 'community of learners'. A collaborative group can develop into a community when its task is seen as a means rather than an end. A low-task orientation does not imply that our participants' motivation to convene was not serious. Their eagerness to meet, their commitment was more oriented towards learning than to fulfill their goal, namely to develop the core-curriculum. This became apparent in the nature of the discourse, which left a lot of space for half-baked ideas to be thrashed out, as well as for personal expressions of feelings.

The three criteria: relationship; equality; and freedom score high in the community. Interpersonal relations and freedom promise a medium in which we can most fully be ourselves. Thus, the community becomes a condition for individuality, whereby people feel they can voice their embryonic ideas without fear of being ridiculed or of breaking the consensus. Reciprocity of freedom and equality implies that roles, positions, status, etc., become latent and do not affect relationship.

This is clearly seen in the case of Uri, who, as a young teacher, is sensitive to the climate of equality and interpersonal relationship within the group irrespective of position, role or status.

The switch of orientation reflected in the third excerpt, occurred not merely with time, but as a result of *practice.* Uri had jumped into deep waters; he had actually tried the new ideas in his classroom and, much to his surprise, he enjoyed it. This explains the strong impact of his monologue on the other participants of the group, it contained a challenge to the others to follow in his footsteps.

Ecological Thinking

I hope that these examples of different groups involved in the process of transforming their school educational orientation will help readers understand what we mean by ecological thinking. Ecological thinking represents an alternative vision of educational change, replacing current top-down and bottom-up models. The latter, based on linear thinking, imply causality as well as power and control. In contrast, ecological thinking involves a circular, collaborative and interactive orientation of learning. It is both the process and the product, with emphasis placed on the double role of all participants, teachers, students, researchers and all those who take part in this learning process.

In justifying the advantages of this new conception over other comparable approaches, let us first look at the assumptions that they hold in common.

The following eight underlying assumptions were identified by Dent and Umpelbee (1998) in the four main traditions of System Science, Cybernetics, Organizational Learning, Total Quality Management, and Operations Research:

(1) Self-Organization: Complex systems organize themselves. In other words, their characteristic structural and behavioral patterns are primarily the result of interactions among the parts of the system.

(2) Observation: 'Reality' is constructed by the observer. In other words, the observer is included within the domain of description, or subjectivity.

(3) Reflexivity: Reflexive systems are composed of knowing subjects continually generating new states (thoughts) about themselves and able to theorize about them and modify themselves accordingly.

(4) Indeterminism: It is inherently impossible to determine the direction of the change.

(5) Environment (or context) has an integral role in the manifestation of a phenomenon (environment-full as compared to environment-free).

(6) Causality: Circular causality as compared to linear causality implies that cause and effect are interchangeable.

(7) Holism: Entity can be best understood by considering it in its entirety; the whole is more than the sum of its parts.

(8) Relationships form the unit of analysis of all traditions of system science, rather than the components of the system.

Let us dwell on the first assumption self-organization, which is, in many ways, includes all of the others. As an open-ended concept, Prigogine saw it as implying that the future evolves from the present and is thus dependent on interactions that have happened and are continually happening (Capra 1996).

As such, self-organization is a 'becoming' process that is both determined and unpredictable.

Self-organization was further elaborated by Maturana and Varela, two neurologists, who regarded it as the basic principle of a living system. Using the term 'autopoietic,' they defined the living system as 'an autopoietic system that originates a recursive enactment of materials by which its structure is constituted' (Maturana and Varela 1998). As an example of an autopoietic system, they give the individual cell. As the simplest living system, the cell is responsible for the structure of its membrane, on the one hand and, on the other, the membrane, by regulating the inflow and outflow of materials, is responsible for the cell's process of living.

The living organism's capacity to preserve itself, is by changing, yet, that which changes is the system's *structure*, whereas that which the autopoietic system maintains is the system's *organization*.

Adopting the above definition of self-organization, we extend it beyond natural systems to include social systems as well. Thus, compared to natural living systems, which are said to be *structurally coupled* when their participants respond or change synchronically, social systems are said to be *semiotically coupled* when their human participants share a system of signs or language. They are coupled both bodily by their interactive actions as well as mentally, by evolving a system of signs, which serve as their shared interpretants for the environment (Pierce in Guddemi 2000).

Semeiotic coupling creates a *community*, and when the participants of a community share their interpretants in conversationing, they develop *a culture*. In this way, the system of signs (or language) which emerges from the community of speakers, develops its own existence, which, in many ways, determines the speakers' way of thinking (Maturana and Varela 1998).

This circular causality typifies our community of learners, which is a self-organizing group, in which participants share their interpretations while conversing.

Coupled semeiotically, they are led by open conversation rather than by predefined goals and objectives. The new understanding, which emerges from their mutual learning process of reflection and knowledge reconstruction, also forms their identity. As a self-organizing group, the community of learners creates its own agenda and assumes responsibility and ownership for its mode of functioning and for its products (Herbst 1976).

Seeing the 'community of learners' as *a context of learning*, where context is an *internal framework* or a locus of meaningful actions (Oers 1999), the participants do not indulge merely in intellectual conversation but are involved in actions as full persons. Uri's example shows that the question, "How to conduct students individual inquiry studies in the classroom?" was not met by a list of skills or methods. Instead, he draws a vivid picture of his teaching experience, disclosing that both teacher and students interact meaningfully as persons. No wonder he characterized it as 'value education'.

As a cultural-historical phenomenon, activity integrates human actions into a coherent whole, forming the basis for meaningful interpretations and actions of the learner. How a person acts on objects demonstrates how he/she stands in the world. Thus, a dialectical relationship between the individual learner as subject, and the ecology of the learning situation, as context, are mutually dependent.

This interrelation between the individual process of learning and that of the group or the community, was beautifully formulated by Davis and Sumara (1997): "As the learner learns, the context changes simply because one of its components changes, and conversely, as the context changes, so does the very identity of the learner."

The dynamic interconnectedness between the individual and the group is clearly illustrated in the last case study: At the beginning, Uri symbolizes the extreme traditional pole, standing against the group's manifested agenda namely, to change the conventional pedagogy into student-centered initiated learning. Yet, the group allows him the space and freedom to voice his ideas without losing face. In the next group meeting, while adhering cognitively to the didactic idea of teamwork, on the affective level, he expresses his feelings, which stem from his personal experience within the team. He is able to voice his appreciation of the group's ability to listen and, at the same time, to share contradictory ideas. Eventually, he becomes the leading figure of the new pedagogy, for the other teachers to try and follow his experience. This does not imply a modeling effect. Each participant teacher has to find his or her personal way of coping with the new learning situation. In fact, in the later stage of the discourse, we hear voices opposing his style, which, they claim, was presented too simplistically.

My point in bringing forth this example is to highlight the dialectical learning process between the individual learner and the learning group, whereby each participant interacts as a person, recruiting his/her personal knowledge, beliefs or basic assumptions. At the same time, the common understanding that emerges within the group, the reconstructed knowledge, forms a new identity. *Ecological thinking implies conceiving this duality of the individual as part of a group.*

By preferring the concept 'ecological thinking' over cybernetic or system thinking, I emphasize my idea of education as an 'organic' rather than a 'technological' productive enterprise – organic systems that promote growth and development.

Chapter 8

An Emergent Theory of Educational Practice

Having defined what I mean by ecological thinking, and being an educationist, not a philosopher, I still have to cope with the problem of how to intergrate the new concept into an educational practice. In this closing chapter, I intend to show that ecological thinking, which emerged from my research practice, should be understood as a theory of 'living education'(Whitehead 1996).

The notion of a living education serves to emphasize the idea of living one's educational philosophy or experiencing one's educational values rather than merely espousing such theories; adopting and teaching them. It implies that professional development is part of personal growth, of creating one's own curriculum in the same way that living implies creating one's own forms of life. Underlying the notion of living education is the assumption of 'theory' being inseperate from action, involving the person as a whole.

A similar idea was expressed by Macmurray who proposed starting from the primacy of the practical, '*to think from the standpoint of action*'.

Justifying the primacy of action over thought he says:

> When we act, sense, perception and judgement are in continuous activity, along with physical movement. When we think, we exclude overt bodily movements at least. Action then, is a full concrete activity of the self in which *all* our capacities are

employed, while thought is constituted by exclusion of some of
our powers and a withdrawal into an activity which is less
concrete and less complete. (Macmurray 1957)

Elaborating on Bateson, Maturana (in what was termed the
'Santiago theory') identified cognition – the process of knowing
– with living, the process of life. Thus, according to Maturana,
cognition is a much broader concept than thinking, involving
perception, emotion and action. Moreover, in the human realm,
cognition also includes language, conceptual thinking and all
other attributes of human consciousness (Capra 1996). Recent
research extends this idea to include the human nervous system,
endocrine system, and the immune system, within a single
cognitive network.

Whether theory or cognition includes action (Whitehead,
Maturana) or vice versa, action includes theory (Macmurray),
my point is that both overcome the Cartesian division between
body and mind.

The main aim of my book is to emphasize the urgent need to
develop ecological thinking as a 'new thinking', which implies *a
rereading of our world*. It means incorporating our conception
of the relationship, between man and enviromemt into our
context or social structures and human action. Developing a
dialectical relation between them would lead to a new conception
of the educational system as a medium and as an outcome of
human practice rather than as an external constraint. The
implications of such a dialectical relation for the individual
teacher are enormous. Instead of being a small cog in a huge
machine, maneuvered by external powers, the teacher, who has
adopted such a conception can see him or herself as being
empowered to act as a responsible agent who can 'make a
difference'.

The book, based on case studies taken from different
educational projects, clearly illustrates our mode of work within
collaborative frameworks consisting of teachers, principals,
researchers and others. The emphasis is on the *process*, the
interplay between theory and practice. Each case is driven by a
focal research question, which is riewed both as authentic and

meaningful to the participants who have identified it. Within a collaborative setting, they indulge in research or data collection and in reflection on their findings.   As a result, new understanding is achieved, which leads to new questions or re-formulation of the original question. It is like stepping on to a platform and seeing a wider view of reality (and a higher degree of complexity). In turn, the platform serves as jumping board for new research endeavors, for the construction of new understanding, and so on.

The book does not aspire to arrive at prescribed solutions, nor at any sort of product that would hint at the right answer or the one-and-only correct way of action. My aim is to open the discourse around what I see as key educational questions, to suggest a possible route of action and, finally, to call interested readers to join in by experimenting tentative ways.

I began my long journey in the early eighties with a small intervention project within the framework of the self-renewal movement of school change. I was at the time intrigued by the concept, 'resistance to change', which was quoted heavily in those days, and decided to study it from within. Today, I see this somewhat naive approach as most sig-nificant in the sense that it opened a new venue for researchers as insiders. Yet, the concepts used, such as 'school self-renewal', 'school resistance to change', and 'educational intervention' were all part of the dominating discourse, whereby schools where talked about as if they were a separate entity, a bounded-off educational system.

School self-renewal as an answer to school-renewal, its parent movement, conveyed the notion of independence with respect to the intrusion of ideas or researchers. Intervention, on the other hand, conveyed the position of researchers, who, as outsiders, aim at introducing change. I remember being annoyed by the connotation of these terms, but then, we are all captives of our language.

The following example reflects our frame of mind at that time: As reported in Chapter 2, we found it difficult to evaluate the project, the extent of the school's self-renewal. I remember our discussions about the need to 'test' the school's self-renewal. We postulated that in order to be able to claim success, we would have to withdraw from the school and give it a chance to cope with future school problems. Only in such a way could it's teachers newly acquired reflective and diagnostic abilities, their independence and autonomy in dealing with school problems, be evaluated.

This example demonstrates the kind of methodological discourse in which we were taking part, as well as the paradigm guiding our work, according to which knowledge is an objective outside entity.

The first signs of our conceptual change stemmed from our reflection on our own action within the project and, as a result, our conception of the whole intervention situation as a system – a system in which we, the research team, were but one subsystem, and where knowledge is generated independently and diffused along unknown and unexpected routes. This change from the top-to-bottom route of knowledge flow, signifies a change of control where, as research team, we were functioning as a part of the situation, and not as sole controllers of the process.

This, I believe, represented an important turning point in professional development, of all who took part in the project, changing their research orientation to become action-researchers. Implicitly, this entailed a change from their linear, sequential idea of change to a non-linear, circular process within a system.

The shift from the micro (a one-school project) to the macro (the educational system) was coupled with another important component: the establishment of collaboration or dialogue with the university. The LAHAV project was not merely a larger setting, consisting of numerous schools, but also a collaborative framework, which provided the space and time for the development of relationships between researchers and teachers.

There was a great deal of information exchanged between schools, exposure to different models and, most importantly, the group gradually became a reflective medium where learning took the form of knowledge reconstruction rather than knowledge transmission.

I believe that I was driven by the need to distance myself from the schools, or rather the sites of the teachers' own initiatives. I felt that they needed their own space or degrees of freedom, and I feared that our presence could disturb their process of development. Today, it is clear that I was still bound to the old paradigm that separates the researcher from her site of research. I was under the influence of the old discourse that regarded such disturbances as 'noise'.

Here, it is perhaps worth mentioning an unexpected effect of our project, namely, its impact on the university's in-service courses for teachers. As a result of our central LAHAV INSET, the department of Education adopted the idea of long-term instead of short-term target inservice courses, to promote further education for teachers, within a framework that accompanies the teachers throughout their working life. Thus, the role of INSET courses gradually shifted from providing new skills or teaching methods, to teachers' professional development.

We saw this as an indication of a conceptual shift with respect to the teaching profession; a shift from the conventional model of the 'instrumental teacher' whose role is to transmit knowledge, to the new model of the 'reflective teacher' whose role is to promote learning and, hopefully, to develop autonomous learners.

As for the school-based (SB) INSETS, they acted as a self-organizing teams, deciding on their topic of inquiry and taking responsibility for their agenda. We were fascinated by the diversity of ideas produced by the different teams, but encouraged them to test their ideas first, before formulating a proposal of change for the management.

However, in all these cases, we conceived ourselves as outside researchers, as uninvolved participants, observing the system. In cybernetic terms, our macro-view of the system was that of first-order cybernetics. I remember using the term 'remote control' when asked to define our role. I did not realize then the full connotation of this definition – neither of 'remote' nor of 'control'.

This leads us to Chapter 3, which relates back to the micro-level and to the group, facilitated by me, and consisting of the entire teaching staff of a 10th grade vocational class. Becoming involved and interacting with the field probably indicates my need as an action researcher to go back to the process of professional development *from within,* to gain deeper insight into the process.

In many respects, the group was a microcosmos reflecting the realities of a large comprehensive school.   By creating a multifaceted reflective context or, put metaphorically, exposing the participants to a 'hall of mirrors', they gradually learned to listen to each other and accept the other's feedback, while lowering the defenses that guarded their preferred image. As a consequence, they developed new insight into their teaching and their students' learning. They now saw teaching not as a linear pre–designed process, but as a complex interactive process involving different systems or subsystems of knowledge.

The ethical implications stemming from this new orientation are that all students, as members of the classroom community, have to have a way to participate in the classroom activities.   In other words, *to learn is to participate in and contribute to the evolution of the communal practice*. Secondly, different interpretations of students are not taken as deficits. Academic success and failure in the classroom are neither an exclusive property of individual students nor of the instruction that they receive. Instead, it is cast as the relation between individual students and practice, they and the teacher construct. This ethical di-mension is important because it brings to the fore the diversity of students' reasoning (Cobb and Bowers 1999).

A frequently used concept 'disciplinary problems' points to a clear disriction between teaching/learning as a main goal, and managing a classroom as a more marginal aspect of the teacher's role. This distiction is emphasized by such practises as that of introducing a counselor into the school system, or in England, by trying to separate from teaching 'pastoral care'. In such systems, teachers are seen as responsible only for teaching, and disciplinary problems became the responsibility of the counselor. I see the concept of disciplinary problems as part of the conventional discourse, which is embedded in the notion of teaching as an act of controlling or 'policing', whereby, we adults force our students to act according to classroom norms of obedience. On this view the assumption is that students' learning runs counter to their natural dispositions or personal interests. Once discipline problems cease to be seen only as a disturbance of order or the breaking of norms, they can begin to be seen as an indication of teachers failure to reach, motivate or interest some of their learners. On this view part and parcel of the teacher's agenda is to make learning attractive to all kinds of learners.

Some signs of development along these lines are discernible in our group learning process. Questions of evaluation as well as punishment, (in response to Ricky's marking system), lead to the new notion of evaluation as a dialogue. Rule-breaking, such as vandalism and theft, are treated by the different teachers within the framework of their respective subject matters. Motivation to learn is understood as internal, stemming from the Mechanics workshop rather than external, stemming from testing or other means of control. I see instances such as these as representing 'buds' of change towards new educational thinking.

The 'explosion' episode was very illuminative in my view. It clearly spelled out the boundaries of what these teachers were prepared to accept as teachers and as persons. Phrases such as 'the teacher as a person' tend to over-simplify or overlook these boundaries. Due to the egalitarian orientation developed during the year, teachers learned to accept differences among the participants rather than politely ignore them. However, this was not extended to include students as equal persons with the right to express their opinions or provide feedback on their joint classroom experience. It seems that there is a deeply buried 'tabu' against students voicing their ideas about their teachers (or elders), which acts like a 'mythological trap' against reason or, in this case, against our espoused theories. Over the years I have become highly aware of these limitations, or boundaries of reflection.

This leads us to Chapter 4, which deals with the need to evaluate the self-renewal project in what we termed, a 'democratic evaluation' framework. Our aim was to illuminate the process of evaluation, mainly for the participating teachers as a first-order audience; to involve them as partners in the process of questioning, reflecting and rethinking their activities within the project.

Two new closely connected key concepts emerge here, 'partnership' and 'dialogue'. Partnership is seen as a necessary condition for promoting a reflective dialogue between the two parties. These two parties, teachers and researchers, are unequal in terms of their expertise and their status; thus it is a partnership based on an equal relationship bet-ween two unequal partners. The question is, "How can these differences be overcome?" "How can they become complementary?" and "How can complementarity become a real asset?"

We were fascinated by the notion of democratic evaluation. It fitted well with our ideology and social orientation in that it recognized the pluralistic nature of our society as well as the right of the school staff to air their own value-laden opinions. Yet, democratic evaluation is an ambiguous concept, one which had rarely been implemented.   With no clear model to follow, we had only our intuition and reflective wisdom to rely on as guiding principles.

Our primary task was to build a climate of mutual trust between the teachers and researchers. We, therefore, refrained from acting as expert evaluators and, instead, made an effort to start from the teachers' point of reference. They had decided to use their own tests to assess their students' achievements. When the result of this assessment proved discouraging, we decided it was time for us to cooperate. By careful analysis, we were able to disclose the complexity of the situation, offer a new interpretation instead of the black-and-white picture they had drawn, and trigger new reframed research questions, which laid the foundation for our reflective dialogue.   The reflective dialogue enhanced the process of self-evaluation, gradually disclosing the link between the teachers' basic assumptions and beliefs, and their teaching behavior. Thus, the process of school evaluation implemented by the school staff as inside evaluators, promoted their personal professional development.

The advantage of such an evaluative framework stems from the complementarity of the two unequal partners. As 'outside evaluators', we had access to formal evaluative knowledge but we could not impose it upon the participating teachers. By promoting them as 'inside evaluators', they could reflect on the consequences of their action. We were sensitive to our partners' vulnerability in the process of evaluation, and we were careful to guard their confidentiality against higher authorities, such as inspectors. This enhanced their trust, leading them to open up and disclose more information, which, in turn, heightened our

insight and deepened our understanding of their role as
professionals.

To conclude, choosing a democratic evaluation model,
emphasizes the evaluator's role as responsible for presenting the
case to those who have to make decisions, in order to facilitate
their final judgment. It does not imply that the evaluator is
neutral in the sense of not voicing his or her personal values.
Democratic evaluation was our choice specifically because this
model advocates pluralism as the name of the game.
Accordingly, each party (including ourselves) is expected and
encouraged to voice his or her ideas explicitly.

In Chapter 5, the focus of our work shifts back to the macro-
level, which is extended to include the school as part of the
community.

Yerucham, a small town in the desert, provided us with the
optimal conditions for learning about the school-environment
relationship or, the community as a learning resource. The
Community Comprehensive school (CCS) idea, stemmed from
our ecological conception, yet we had no intention of imposing
our ideas top-down on the school staff. Instead, we involved our
partners in the deliberation of what they meant by community
school. The new concept of the CCS was thus jointly
constructed.

The first step, initiated by our industry partners, was to suggest
a 'system model' as opposed to the 'apprentice model', which
predominates Israeli vocational education. The metaphor, 'a
factory as a system' was picked up by the the team facilitator and
applied as the main principle of the new vocational curriculum.
This was a huge step forward in our thinking. It also illustrates
what I mean by peer-learning in a collaborative group, of reconstructing their own model of a Community-Comprehensive
school, based on our joint practice. Moreover, the new model
evidently made sense to the participants and, as such, was an
indication of their conceptual change.

Another achievement of the CCS project was the construction
of the interactive double locus model of teachers' conceptual
change. This framework was not new; we had used it all along
but the reflective context, consisting of simple community people

as partners, sharpened our insight into the cardinal contribution of heterogeneity to peer-learning. The dialectical process of reflection in the group gave birth to the new concept, 'community of learners'.

The sixth chapter follows naturally: The 'Desert and Desertification' project is part of a national move towards the integration of science and technology with society (STS); in other words, a shift from a disciplinary to   interdisciplinary orientation. The emphasis of STS on the social context suggests a far more complex relationship between Man and the environment. Where, science and technology, as important aspects of our modern society, are tightly connected with genuine social as well as environmental problems.

The explicit aim of the STES project was to develop new curriculum units, which would broaden awareness and responsibility toward real social and environmental problems. The STES project provided a new venue to apply our alternative, ecological conception.   It was an opportunity to liberate environmental education from its predominantly positivistic orientation, whereby the natural environment is isolated and its so-called 'equilibrium' protected against human scientific and technological interventions.   Instead, true to the modern ecological orientation, human interaction and involvement is accepted as fundamental principle of environmental education (EE) or STS, and values such as personal responsibility and participation become our primary educational goal.

This laid the basis for our new concept, 'ecological thinking', which emphasizes the contemporary ecological conception of open systems.

The two case studies described in Chapters 5 and 6 aimed at extending the educational system beyond the school; in the CCS project by creating a partnership with different institutions and developing a meaningful dialogue with community people.   In Sdeh-Boker, which is not an ordinary community but a university campus, the partners were all researchers and some of them were also parents. The dialectical tension, which developed between researchers and teachers as practitioners, was another important contribution to the learning process. It all added to our understanding of the dynamic mutual learning process that takes place within a 'community of learners', generating professional knowledge as well as professional development of the participants.

Chapter 7 unfolds the ultimate version of my educational thinking namely, what do I mean by 'new thinking in education'. Ecological thinking is introduced first by three examples drawn from my field of action. What clearly emerges from the three different case studies are the following basic principles that underlie Ecological Thinking (ET):

  * The 'community of learners', as a self-organizing group, is a necessary medium for the process and product of ET. Characterized by high relationship, equality and freedom, the community becomes a condition for individuality.
  * It follows, that a mutual dependency exists within the 'community of learners', between the individual learner as subject and the ecology of the learning situation as context; a dialectical relationship between the individual process of learning and that of the group or the community.
  * The emphasis of ecological thinking is on the double role of participants, as actors and reflectors. Interacting with other components within, and reflecting on the system and their interaction from without, ultimately, makes them aware and responsible for understanding, for knowledge construction, and for action.
  * Like cogwheels that rotate each other, a mutual learning process is enhanced in such collaborative frameworks of learning, consisting of teachers and their students. These frameworks should be extended to include other parties, such as researchers, parents, administrators, and all those who form part of the educational system.
  The bottom line is *mutuality or dialectics* between the individual learner and his or her context; between process and product; structure and function, and between participation and acquisition as metaphors of learning; all these constitute the 'new thinking', which I claim is necessary for educational change.

How to Make Ecological Thinking into a Theory of 'Living Education'

The challenge of this concluding chapter is to show how to live this new educational metaphor – how to actually experience the underlying values and to integrate professional development as part of personal growth.

Committed to the idea of theory and action as non-separable, and the primacy of practice, I intuitively turned to action in order to find a solution. Naturally, the starting point had to be a 'community of learners', and the most obvious candidates were my graduate students, past and present. I presented the idea to them and managed to attract five or six interested participants. We formed a group and tried to define ourselves and our goals, but soon decided unanimously against definitions. For want of a better title, we chose 'Discourse Group' as our name.   We decided to meet every other week, and after the first year, changed it to longer sessions once every three weeks. All of our deliberations are recorded and participants take turns to transcribe and e-mail the proceeedings to all members, ensuring enough time to read and reflect on the text before the next meeting. Our common denominator is obviously our active involvement in educational or social change.   In fact, all participants act also as facilitators of groups of students, teachers, school principles or community representatives. Altogether, we represent a whole spectrum of fields of action.

We have entered our fourth year, with only a small turnover of participants (one left, one returned and two new members joined). We adhere to the norms of "no predefined agenda, of being led by an open conversation out of which different issues and key concepts emerge, of maintaining a facilitative climate that does not eliminate critical reflection". At some point last year, I drew a diagram of our community of learners on the blackboard in my office (see Figure 8.1) where our meetings take place. The drawing is still there, now embellished by alterations added by participants from time to time.

Figure 8.1: The Discoursen group

Legend: Participants A,B,C,D,E,F are interactive 'insiders' as
well as reflective 'outsiders' (A', B', C', D', E', F')

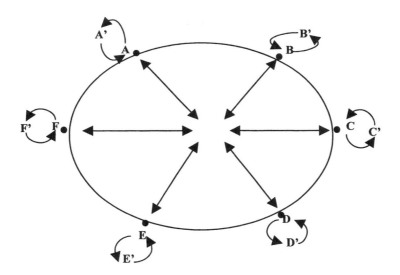

A significant development of the group, was voiced only
recently:

> - I remember that in our first year, I felt obliged to participate.
> Today, I feel the group is so much part of me, I cannot miss it,
> otherwise how can I explain my regular attendance. In the same
> way, I strongly feel the absence of any one of you.

The opportunity to answer the question, "What is the
significance of the group?" or "What does the group mean to
you? came with the arrival of the new members, who openly
asked for explanations such as, "What is it all about?"

The following responses serve to map the participants' conception of the 'discourse group. (The excerpt is taken from the group meeting held on 2.4.2001.)

P. - I am interested in hearing what you do; what you talk about.

E. - Our group work is a kind of constructivist discourse in which we try to inquire, to study what a Constructivist discourse means.... There are two parallel processes, one is to keep on reflecting on the group process, and the other is to add new concepts and test their relevancy for the participants...

S. - We are constantly trying to deal with the question whether the group interaction that we call, 'community of learners' is a necessary prerequisite.

E. - I would add that it is a kind of effort to construct new knowledge on the basis of our experience.

N. - A dialogue between what happens to me here and what happens in my group in the field, as two parallel processes.

Y. -Compared to all other learning contexts, there is no goal or objectives here. We have all the time in the world... It took me some time to understand what really happens here. I believe this is real learning. You flow on with the group, without constraints, and realize that something has been generated.

E. - Our presence here signifies an effort to understand and, at the same time, it provides the oppotunity to make a difference. It implies a kind of responsibility as to what parts of oneself one decides to contribute to the common discourse.

D. - At the beginning, we were occupied by the question of what do we do here. What you have just heard is a product of a long process. I would add that we have created an open medium where participants feel free to act as they choose. I see it as an indication of a high degree of liberty.

P. (the newcomer, has a request to the group): - Have you built a model, for the facilitator, consisting of stages in the process...

N. - I wouldn't go to a one-model-only process. We assume that the direction of development, and even the structure, depend very much on the kind of interactions within the group.

Y. - The conclusion that emerges maybe disheartening ... that each such process is unique.

N. - Even if we have not reached a model, there are many insights, understandings that have grown from the process. For example, for the group to develop, each participant has to identify his or her needs or interests. Being an active participant contributes not only to the group's development but also to the progress and growth of the individual.

E. - We have gained insights, for example, into our ability to lead the process in real-time and, at the same time, to understand it. In our terms, to be an insider and an outsider.

S. - It seems to me your request for a model consisting of stages is contradictory to your work. You have chosen to collaborate with a High Tech industry in order to expose your students to the future, to uncertainty and ambiguity. Yet you ask for a model that would take you backwards...

I hope this excerpt illustrates how participants view or understand our 'discourse group'. It is time now to follow up its function, specifically with regards to our questions on "*how to live ecological thinking; how to experience it*". To cope with these questions I chose to present two episoded from our group process.

The First Example:

Dalia teaches in a Teacher Education college. In her course entitled, 'Problems in the Natural Environment', half of the students are Jewish females and half are Arab Bedouin males. This reflects the Israeli educational system whereby women are dominant in the Jewish sector and men, in the Arab, Bedouin sector. Since the establishment of the State of Israel, its Bedouin population has experienced a continuous transition from their nomadic way of life, living in tents with no formal education, to a more Western mode of life. The transition has been accompanied by numerous crises, mainly due to the confrontation between the young, modern and educated generation and their traditional tribal elders.

Dalia relates the following episode to the 'discourse group':

D. - Only half of the class arrived and I could not teach according to plan. As I hesitated, thinking about how to proceed, the students initiated a conversation focused on the question of our role as teachers. The Bedouin students, who are usually passive, were voicing their problems, complaining about the low status of teachers in their society, about parents beeing abusive toward teachers, and many negative aspects of Bedouin society such as the notion of 'family honor', etc. I kept quiet all through the conversation, careful not to slide into my teacher's role, trying to understand what was happening. After the lesson, I asked some Jewish participants for feedback. They responded very positively, saying, "They (the Bedouins) sit next to us yet we don't know anything about them, about their lives". I, too, felt that something interesting has happened by the mere fact that they had opened up and disclosed their problems in public. But where do I go from there?

The group is quick to respond:

Y. - It seems to me that at least the Jewish students advocate a change. Instead of continuing according to plan, you could use these authentic problems, raised by the Bedouin students, to introduce change in your teaching methods. This could improve their understanding of the concept of 'problems'...

D. - Changing the subject would require a change in the course title.

S. - You could leave the name and change your teaching methods or, alternatively, instead of 'Problems in the Natural Environment', change it to 'Problems in the Human Environment'. Studying the urban system is so much more relevant to your students, and to theirs.

N. - Maybe find a new definition for the term 'Natural Environment'. There is no such thing today as a natural environment without a human presence. Human presence is an integral part of the landscape. It is therefore perfectly legitimate to introduce social problems into a discussion of the environment.

Encouraged by the group, Dalia opened her next meeting with her class by talking about what has happened in the previous lesson, sharing her indecision concerning what course of action to take. A lively discussion followed in which she did not interfere, leaving space for her to make decisions. She gave them an assignment to be carried out in mixed pairs, each pair choosing a topic raised in the discussion, and approaching it from their different perspectives.

One student complains: "I came to learn Geography and I thought the first lessons were really interesting. As for our 'teacher problems', there are plenty of other frameworks where these can be discussed".

In the next meeting of the discourse group, the participants approach Dalia wanting to hear what has happened in her classroom since.

E. - Tell us what kind of change you have gone through.

D. - I am very happy with the process. I gained the legitimation and courage to consider teaching differently. This could not have happened without the group... I am not sure whether it is for the better or the worse. It might just remain a fleeting experience and nothing more...

E. - I wanted to know how *you* felt.

D. - Yes, I know the answer. I hate myself in the teacher's role, when they all wait passively for me to transfer knowledge. It was not easy to admit this.

E. - I could sense something when I saw the change in your expression ... your eyes... I believe you could benefit from a deeper understanding of why ... how it relates to you personally.

Dalia had already expressed her interest in the discourse group to apply the group's learning climate in her own classroom. She was keen to move away from the conventional didactic-model, where learning is organized and directed by the teacher's pre-determined goals, to a new setting, one that gives space for the students' different learning venues, different interests.

Her first step is to react differently to the student-initiated conversation, by listening carefully to their voices, legitimizing their stories, and helping them formulate their implicit interests into a path of inquiry. This is not a simple step. She is confronted with conflicting reactions, some encouraging but others reminding her of her 'mandate' as a teacher. The story highlights the mutuality of learning between our group as a community of learners, and Dalia's classroom. Our group helps her sort out her own needs in terms of her role as a teacher. She begins to articulate her feelings of hating the authoritative role of the teacher as a resource for knowledge, realizing that she feels good in her new role of a teacher who facilitates students' autonomous learning. This is but a first step. Dalia is not sure she can follow the new path. Subjectively, she is able to listen and accept her students as persons without necessarily having to agree with their views, which is a most important step forward.

The group discourse can be seen as a multi-voiced discourse, as opposed to one-voice consensus or brainwashing. Each participant approaches from his or her unique reference point. The result is a richly colored conversation. It is not a trivial conversation. It relays a clear message of change of action, connected to reason and a deeper understanding.

The Second Example

Eti is an experienced Organizational Developer. Her story is about a collaboration with a group of orthodox religious Jews in an attempt to improve their school-parent relationship. One of the major internal conflicts in Israel is between its secular Jewish population, with its democratic Zionist aims, and the extreme religious sector, who are not Zionists and who would prefer Israel to be a theocractic state. 'Chabad' is one such extreme religious non-Zionist sect.

Eti recounts in the group how she was approached by the principal of a Chabad boys' school asking her help. The parents of the community were critical of the school curriculum and were threatening to intervene. The principal's aim was to establish an effective framework for positive parent involvement in the school. Eti continues:

E. - This is an experience between me and me...I believe one can work with people who adhere to a different faith without trying to change them...I see it as a challenge... As an organizational developer, I feel I can help them build a system that will help them improve their functioning without disturbing their faith. I mean to work with them without trying to change them, first, because I cannot, and secondly, because I don't want to . I want to build something valuable for them, and for me, based on their values.

N. - I don't understand your approach.

E. - For me, this is the meaning of constructivism; to accept the fact they have different assumptions, and respect them. I believe we termed this, 'multi-culturalism'.

Eti continued with her meetings, which she described in rather surrealistic terms: "one sole woman with a team of five men, all with long beards and wearing black traditional robes". She admits that contrary to her pre-conceptions, they seemed open-minded and sincere, sharing their difficulties in the team.

After a few weeks, she introduces the issue again in the 'discourse group':

E. - I confess, I have learned to appreciate these people, to like them. I couldn't have done it without the help of the Rabbi, a most enlightening person.

N. - Your example of working with a group whose way of life is totally different makes an interesting story.

S. - You managed to substitute their fighting attitude with respect to the parents, to a collaborating approach. You represented a feminine approach as opposed to their masculine one.

E. - My idea was to combine the two into a new conception beneficial for both of us.

J. - Don't you see that it strengthens their framework?

E. - It looks fine to me. It's in no way against my professional principles.

J. - I can see that theoretically your case is interesting. As an outsider, you satisfy your curiosity. But where does it leave you on the ideological level?

E. - I admit, this question has bothered me lately. I thought that as an organizational facilitator I could use my profesional tool disregarding my beliefs.

S. - Could you elaborate here? What is your role conception?

E. - I feel I have a dilemma here. I help people who stand in a complete opposite position with regard to my values, and I am actually empowering them. You see, I looked at it as a professional experience...

Eti feels enthusiastic about her new experience with the Chabad team. When the group points out the discrepancy between her personal beliefs and basic assumptions, and those of the Chabad, she hides behind labels such as 'multi-culturalism' and 'constructivism'. It is apparent that as the professional facilitator of that group, she conceives her role from the outside. In cybernetic terms, she acts on a first-order level, looking at the internal interactions in the group from the outside, denying the 'inter-influence' between herself and the orthodox male group.

The facilitator's role, a relevant issue to all participants of our group, is the issue at stake. How far can one stretch one's objectivity, keep acting within the 'role' without touching the 'person'?

The discourse group seems to be reacting patiently, waiting for her further experience to trigger her reflection. The first 'crack' in Eti's armour comes as a result of the closer personal relationship developed between herself and the orthodox participants. Seeing them as subjects rather than objects, or in other words, developing an inter-subjective relationship led to new insights. Confusion triggered her to reflect critically on the absurd situation of empowering the orthodox school staff, contrary to her own ideology and strong personal beliefs.

This case brought Eti to develop a deeper understanding of the mutual learning process of the individual and the group. Influenced by Buber and Bachtin's writings, she adopted the term 'subjectivity' to describe our participation in the mutual learning process within the community of learners, as both inside learners and outside reflectors. Acting as subjects and not objects, the discourse involves participants as 'whole persons', and not only the cognitive domain. When subjectivity is applied to the facilitator, it entails a change of his or her role, from an objective neutral professional towards a subjective whole person. By conceptualizing this inter-subjective discourse between members of a 'community of learners', new understanding of the group as a learning context is constructed.

I hope these episodes have succeeded in demonstrating what I mean by 'living our philosophy', in this case, our metaphor, ecological thinking. I hope they have also clarified the prerequisite of a 'community of learners' as an optimal framework for exercising and promoting ecological thinking. Within this medium, participants are coupled semeiotically; they change synchronically with respect to each other.   Each participant within the community is coupled bodily by the mutual interactive actions, and mentally, by evolving a language serving as their shared interpretants for the environment (Maturana and Varela 1998).

The new understanding, that emerged from our mutual learning process, formed our new language. For example, concepts such as 'self-organizing-system', or 'subjectivity', encountered in the literature and understood theoretically, after being thrashed out in the group conver-sation, became personally meaningful and a part of our language system. As such, they also changed our identity.

This is a completely different discourse from the one based on 'technical rationality', which   still dictates our educational discourse. Moving from the micro case study to the macro system, we find that our current educational theories are highly influenced by the global market economy. Schools are compared to business organizations. Concepts from the marketplace such as 'productivity', 'competition', and 'efficiency' have replaced the more human discourse about ethics and responsibility. I believe it is time to move away from 'production models' and start thinking in terms of 'growth models' because, to quote Franklin (1992), " if there ever was a growth process that cannot be divided into rigid predetermined steps, it is education"

Nature at large turns out to be more like human nature – unpredictable, sensitive to the surrounding world, influenced by small fluctuations. Accordingly, the appropriate way to approach nature is not through domination and control, but through respect, cooperation and dialogue.   In the living world of dissipative structures, history plays an important role, the future is uncertain, and such uncertainty lies at the heart of creativity.(ibid)

By preferring the concept, Ecological-Thinking to Cybernetic or System Thinking, I emphasize my idea of education as an organic rather than a technological productive enterprise. Organic systems promote growth and development; they are comparable to highly complex systems or 'multilevel webs' (Hardy 2001).   Hardy actually uses the small group as an example of a multilevel web. The other example is the human mind,   both represent sites for multidimensional interactions. Thus, each person in the group, being a multilevel system, experiences simultaneous and interacting processes, belonging to different levels, such as feelings, sensations, fantasies, desires, intellectual ideas, reasoning, actions, etc. All these interact with similar processes in the systems of the other members of the group. In this way the social web embeds the multilevel organization of its members, and carry on the multilevel dynamic interactions between numerous variables (Bertalanffy 1967).

One last word about educational change: I began this book with the image of a 'grandfather clock' whose rotating cogwheels represent the various components of the educational system. The image of cogwheels mutually rotating one another symbolized interactive and circular as opposed to linear causality. To bring about educational change, all parties, teachers, students, researchers, parents, community representatives and, most importantly, administrators or policy makers-need to be drawn into the discourse. Like cogwheels mutually rotating one another, they become involved in a mutual educational 'poly-textual discourse'. This is how I imagined we could achieve a systemic educational change.

Today, however, I am more sensitive to the limitations of this image due to the fixed structure of a clock, unadapted to dynamic unforeseen venues of change. I hope I have convinced the reader that the image of a 'multilevel web' of interactions or inter-influences between a large and indefinite of forces, is a more appropriate metaphor for motivating systemic educational change.

Bibliography

Anderson, G.J. *The assessment of LEI.* Halifax, Nova Scotia: Atlantic Institute of Education, 1973.

Argyris, C. and Schon, D.A. *Organizational Learning.* Reading, Mass., Addison Wesley, 1978.

Aviram, A and Keiny, S. Enhancing autonomy: The school, the teacher and the student. Unpublished paper, 1992.

Avraham, A. *Le Monde Interieur des Enseignants.* Paris: Epi Editeurs, 1972.

Bamberger, J. and Schon, D.A. "Learning as Reflective Conversation with Materials: Notes from Work in Progress". *Art Education*, March, 1983.

Bateson, G. *Steps to an Ecology of mind.* London: Granada Press, 1972.

Belenky, M.F., Clinchy, B.M., Goldberg, N.R. and Tarule, J. M. *Women's ways of Knowing: The development of Self, Voice and Mind.* New-York: Basic Books, 1986.

Bernstein, B. *Pedagogy symbolic control and identity. Theory, research, ctitique.* London: Taylor & Francis, 1996.

Bertalanffy, L. *Robots men and mind.* New-York: George Braziller, von 1967.

Capra, F. *The web of life.* Anchor books, Doubleday, 1996.

Carr, W. and Kemmis, S. *Becoming Critical: Knowing Trough Action Research.* Victoria: Deakin University Press, 1983.

Carr, W. and Kemmis, S. *Becoming critical: Education, knowledge & action research.* London: Falmer Press, 1986.

Clandinin, J.D. "Personal practical knowledge: A study of classroom images". *Curriculum Inquiry*, 1985.

Cobb, P. "Where is the mind? Constructivist and sociocultural perspectives on mathematical development". *Educational Researcher* 23(7) (1994): 13-20.

Cobb, P. and Bowers. "Cognitive and situated learning perspectives in theory and practice". *Educational Researcher* 28(2) (1999): 4-10.

Cronbach, L.J. and Associates. 1980. *Towards Reform of Program Evaluation: Aims Methods and Institutional Arrangements.* San Francisco. CA: Jossey Bass, 1980.

Davis, M.B. "Climatic instability, time lag, and community disequilibrium". In *Community Ecology*, edited by Diamond, J and Case, T.J. New York: Harper & Row (1986): 269-284.

Davis, B. and Sumara, D. J. "Cognition Complexity and Teacher Education". *Harvard Educational Review* 67(1) (1997): 105-125.

Dent, E.B. and Umpleby, S.A. "Underlying assumptions of several traditions in systems science". In *Cybernetics and Systems '98*, edited by Trapple, R. vol. 1. Austrian society for Cybernetic studies, 1998.

Duit. R. "Conceptual change approaches in science education". *Conceptual Change.* A paper presented at Jena, 1994.

Ebbutt, D. and Elliott, J. "Why school teachers do research? " In *Issues in Teaching for Understanding*, edited by Ebbutt, D. and Elliott, J. Cambridge Institute of Education, 1985.

Elbaz, F. "The teacher's practical knowledge: Report of a case study". *Curriculum Inquiry* 11(1) (1981): 43-71.

Elliott, J. *Action Research for Educational Change. Developing Teachers & Teaching Series*. Open University Press, 1992.

———. *Developing hypotheses about classroom, from teachers practical constructs*. Ford Teaching Project . Cambridge Institute of Education, 1981.

———. "Educational theory and the professional learning of teachers: An overview". *Cambridge Journal of Education* 19(1) (1989): 81-101.

Faital, A. and Keiny, S. "A case study of teachers professional development". In *Theoretical and Practical Implications of Research on Teachers Thinking: Proceedings of the International Conference on Teachers Thinking*. Israel, Beer-Sheva, 1990.

Fenstermacher, G. "The known and the unknown: the nature of knowledge in research on teaching". *Review of Research in Education* 20 (1994): 3-56.

Fielding, M. "Beyond collaboration: On the importance of community". In *Consorting and Collaboration in the Education Market Place*, edited by Bridges, D. and Husband, C. Falmer Press, 1995.

Fielding, M. "How and why learning styles matter: Valuing difference in teachers and learners". In *Differentiation in the secondary curriculum*, edited by Hart, S. Routledge, 1996.

Foerster, H. von "Ethics and second order cybernetics". *Cybernetics & Human Knowing* 1(1) (1992): 9-19.

Frankenstein, C. *Impaired Intelligence*. New York: Gordon and Breach, 1970.

Franklin, U. "The real world of Mathematics, Science and Technology Education". A paper based on an address at an *Invitational Colloquium by the MSTE group*. Queen's University, 16-17 May 1991.

French, W. and Bell, C. *Organizational development.* Toronto: Prentice Hall, 1973.

Fullan, M. Miles, M. B. and G. Taylor, G. "Organizational development in schools: the state of art". *Review of Educational Research* 50 (1980): 121-183.

Glasersfeld, E. "Learning as a constructive activity". In *Problems of representation in teaching and Learning of Mathematics*, edited by Janvier, C. Hillsdale NJ: Lawrence Elbaum Ass. (1987): 3-17.

———."Cognition, construction of knowledge and teaching". *Syntheses*, 80(1) (1989): 121-140.

———. "Constructivism reconstructed: A reply to Sutchting". *Science and Education* 1 (1992): 379-384.

Glassberg, S. and Oja, S.N. "A developmental model for enhancing teachers' personal and professional growth". *Journal of Research and Development in Education* 14 (1981): 59-70.

Goodson, I. *Studying Teachers' Lives.* London: Routledge, 1992.

Gore, J.M. and Zeichner, K.M. "Action research and reflective teaching in preservice   teacher education: A case study from the USA". *Teacher and Teacher Education* 7(2) (1991): 119-136.

Gorodetsky, M. and Keiny, S. "Curriculum development in Science Technology and Society (STS) as a means of teachers' conceptual change". *Educational Action Research* 4(2) (1996): 185-195.

Gorodetsky, M. and Keiny, S. "Participative learning and conceptual change". In *Reframing the Process of Conceptual Change* edited by Limon, M. and Mason, L. Kluwer Press, 2002.

Gorodetsky, M. Keiny, S and Hoz, R. "Conceptions, practice and change". *Educational Action Research* 5(3) (1997): 423-433.

Guddemi, P. "Autopoisis, Semeiosis, Co-coupling: A rational language for describing Communication and Adaptation". *Cybernetics and Human Knowing*, 7(2-3) (2000): 127-145.

Handal, G. and Lauvis, P. *Promoting reflective teaching: Supervision in action*. Milton Keynes: Open University Press, 1987.

Hardy, C. "Self-Organization, self-reference and inter-influences in Multilevel Webs: Beyond causality and determinism". *Cybernetics and Human Knowing* 8(3) (2001): 35-59.

Hargreaves, A. *Changing teachers changing times: teachers' work and culture in the postmodern age*. London: Cassell, 1994.

Harries-Jones, P. A *Recursive Vision: Ecological Understanding and Gregory Bateson*. Toronto: University of Toronto Press, 1995.

Herbst, P.D. *Alternatives for Hierarchy*. Holland: Nijhoff, 1976.

Hofstein, A. Ben-Zvi, R. and Carmeli, M. "Classroom behavior of exemplary and non-exemplary chemistry teachers". *Research in Science and Technology Education*, 1990.

Hofstein, A. Gluzman, R. Ben-Zvi, R. and Samuel, D. "A comparative study of chemistry students' perception of the learning environment, in high schools and vocational schools". *Journal of Research in Science Teaching* 8(2) (1990): 185-193.

House, E. "Assumptions underlying evaluation models". *Educational Researcher* 7(3) (1978): 4-12.

Keiny, S. "Action research in the school: a case study". *Cambridge Journal of Education* 15 (1985): 155-161.

——. "Enhancing teachers' professional development through a dialectical process of reflection". *Studies in Education* (1987): 119-140. (in Hebrew)

——. "School-based curriculum development as a process of teachers' professional development". *Educational Action Research* 1(1) (1993): 65-93.

Keiny, S. and Dreyfus, A. "School evaluation as a dialogue between researchers and practitioners". *Studies in Educational Evaluation* 19 (1993):281-295.

Keiny, S. and Dreyfus, A. "Teachers' self-reflection as a prerequisite to their professional development". *Journal of Education for Teaching* 15(1) (1989): 53-63.

Keiny, S. Orion, E. Yahav, I and Shachak, M. *Sdeh Boker Version of Environmental Education.* Sdeh-Boker campus, internal publication, 1982.

Keiny, S., Kushnir, T. and Dreyfus, A. "A model for enhancing teachers' divergent thinking". In *Preservice and Inservice Education of Science Teachers* edited by Tamir, P., Hofstein, A., Ben Peretz, M., Feinstein, B., Finegold, M, Keiny, S. and Sabar, N. Rehovot: Balaban International Science Service, 1983.

Kessels, J.P.A.M. and Korthagen, F.A.J. "The relationship between theory and practice: Back to the classics". *Educational Researcher* 25(3) (1996): 17-22.

Kolb, D.A. and Fry, D. "Towards an applied theory of experimental learning". In. *Theories of Group Processes* edited by Cooper, C.L. New York: Wiley, 1975.

Kuhn, T.S. *The Structure of Scientific Revolutions.* (3rd edn) Chicago: University of Chicago Press, 1962.

Lewy, A. "School evaluation and school autonomy". In *Autonomy in education* edited by Friedman, Y. Jerusalem: Henrietta Szold Institute, 1989. (in Hebrew)

Linder, C.J. "A challenge to Conceptual Change". *Science Education* 77 (1993): 293-300.

Lorti, D. *Schoolteacher.* University of Chicago Press 1975.

MacDonald, B. "Accountability, standarts and the process of schooling". In *Accountability in Education* edited by Becher, T. and Maclure, S. Windsor: NFER Pub.CO.,1978 .

MacDonald, B. Jenkins, D. Kemmis, S, and Tawney, D. *The Program at Two: Evaluation Report on the National Development Programme in Computer Assisted Learning.* Norwich: CARE, East Anglia University, 1975.

Macmurray, J. *The self as an Agent.* Humanity Press International, 1957.

Marton, F. "Phenomenography – a search approach to investigate different understandings of reality". *Journal of Thought* 21 (1986): 28-49.

Marton, F. and Booth, S. *Learning and Awareness.* Mahwah: Lawrence Elbaum Press, 1997.

Maturana, H. R. "Biology of cognition". In *Autopoiesis and Cognition: The realization of the Living,* edited by Maturana, H.R. and Varela, J.J. Dordrecht: Reide, 1980.

Maturana, H. R. "Reality: The search for objectivity, or the quest for a compelling argument". In the ASC workbook: *Language, Emotion, the Social and the Ethical.* Washington University Press, 1992.

Maturana, H.R. and Varela, F.J. *The Tree of Knowledge: The biological roots of human understanding.* Boston & London: Shambhala, 1998.

Miles, M. B. and Fullan, M. "Organization development in schools". In *Small Groups and Personal Change,* edited by Smith.P.B. London: Methuen, 1980.

Miller, A. "Tunnel vision in environmental management". *The Environ-mentalist,* 1982.

Morris, B. *Objectives and Perspectives in Education: Studies in Educational Theory (1955-1970).* London: Routledge and Kegan Paul, 1972.

Oers, B. "From context to contextualization". *Instruction & Learning* 8(6) (1998): 473-488.

Park, P. "People, knowledge, and change in participatory research". *Management Learning* 30(2) (1999): 141-157.

Parllet, M. and Hamilton, D. "Evaluation as illumination: A new approach to the study of innovatory programmes". In *Beyond the Numbers Game,* edited by Hamilton, D et al.,1977. London: Macmillan, 1972.

Posner, G.J, Strike, K.A, Hewson P.W and W. A. Gertzog. "Accommodation of a scientific conception: towards a theory of conceptual change". *Science Education* 24(7) (1982): 211-227.

Prawat, R. S. "Misreading Dewey: Reform, Projects, and the language game". *Educational Researcher* 24(7) 13-22, 1995.

Reshef, S. "School autonomy – A new area in public education". In *Autonomy in Education*, edited by Friedman, Y. Jerusalem: Henrietta Szold Institute, 1989 (in Hebrew)

Richardson, V. "Significant and worthwhile change in teaching practice". *Educational Researcher* 19(7) (1990): 10-18.

Sarason, S. B. *The Culture of the School and the Problem of Change.* Boston: Allyn and Bacon, 1971.

Schmuck, R.A. and Runkel, R.J. *Handbook of Organizational Development in Schools.* Palo Alto, California: Mayfield, 1974.

Schmuck, R. A. Murray, D. Schwartz, M. and Runkel, M. *Consultation for innovative schools: OD for multiunit structure.* Eugene Ore.: Center for Educational Policy and Management, 1975.

Schon, D.A. *The Reflective Practitioner.* London: Temple Smith, 1983.

Schon, D. A. "The theory of inquiry: Dewey's legacy to Education". *Curriculum Inquiry* 22(2) (1992): 119-39.

Schwab, J.J. "Structure of the disciplines: Meanings and significances". In *The structure of knowledge and the curriculum* edited by G.W. Ford, G. W and Pugno, L. Chicago: Rand McNally, 1964.

Sfard, A. "On two metaphors of learning and the danger of choosing just one". *Educational Researcher* 27(2) (1998): 4-13.

Shulman. L. S. "Knowledge and teaching: The foundation of a new reform". *Howard Education Review* 57 (1) (1987): 1-22.

Simon, H. *Getting to Know Schools in Democracy: The Politics and Processes of Evaluation.* Falmer Press, 1987.

Smith, J. "Teachers as collaborative learners in clinical supervision: A state-of-the-art review". *Journal of Education for Teaching* 10(1) (1984): 24-38.

Somekh, B. "Inhabiting each other's castles: Towards knowledge and mutual growth through collaboration". *Educational Action Research* 2(3) (1995): 351-378.

Stake, R.E. *The countenance of educational evaluation.* Teachers College Records, 1967.

Steffe, L.P. and Gale, J.E. *Constructivism and Education.* Lawrence Elbaum Press, 1995.

Stenhouse, L. *An Introduction to Curriculum Research and Development.* London: Heinemann, 1975.

Stenhouse, L.,Verma, G.K., Wild, R.D. and Nixon, J. *Teaching about Race Relation: Problems and Effects.* London: Routledge and Kegan Paul, 1982.

Van Manen, M. "Linking ways of knowing with ways of being practical". *Curriculum Inquiry* 6 (1977): 205-228.

Waks, L. "Citizenship in transition: Globalization, postindustrial technology and education". An MSTE lecture presented at the symposium *Life after school: Education, globalization and the person* Canada: Queens University, April 1995.

Walberg, H.J. and Anderson, G.H. "Classroom climate and individual learning". *Journal of Educational Psychology* 59 (1968): 414-419.

Watzlawick, P. Weakland, J.H. and Fisch. *Change: Principles of Problem Formation and Problem Resolutions.* New York: Norton, 1974.

Whitehead, J. "Living educational theories and living contradictions: a Response to Mike Newby". *Journal of Philosophy of Education* 30(3) (1996): 457-461.

Wilson, S. Shulman, S and Richert, A. "150 different ways of knowing: Representations of knowledge in teaching". In *Exploring teachers thinking*, edited by Calderhead, J. London: Cassell Educational, 1987.

Zamir, J. and Keiny, S. "School innovations as a means of teachers personal development: A case study of a teacher". In *Theoretical and Practical Implications of Research on Teachers Thinking*. Proceedings of the International Conference on Teachers Thinking. Israel, Beer-Sheva, 1980.

Zeichner, K.M. "Research on teacher thinking and different views of reflective practice". In *Research in Teacher Thinking and Practice*, edited by Carlgren, Handal, G. and Vaage, S., 1993.

INDEX

236